CRAZY BRAVE

Michael Gurr

Current Theatre Series
Currency Press • Sydney
in association with
Playbox Theatre, Melbourne

CURRENT THEATRE SERIES

First published in 2000
by Currency Press Pty Ltd,
PO Box 2287, Strawberry Hills, NSW, 2012, Australia
enquiries@currency.com.au
www.currency.com.au
in association with Playbox Theatre, Melbourne

NATIONAL LIBRARY OF AUSTRALIA CIP DATA
Gurr, Michael, 1961–.
Crazy brave.
ISBN 0 86819 615 0.
1. Urban warfare—Victoria—Melbourne—Drama.
I. Playbox Theatre (Melbourne, Vic.). II. Title.
(Series: Current theatre series).
A822.3

Set by Dean Nottle
Printed by Southwood Press, Marrickville

Contents

For Kerry Walker

Crazy Brave was first produced by Playbox Theatre, Melbourne, and performed at The C.U.B. Malthouse on 28 June 2000, with the following cast:

ALICE FORD	Alison Whyte
PAUL ARNOTT	James Wardlaw
DEBORAH DEE	Fiona Todd
HAROLD HOFFMAN	Bruce Myles
NICK FEAST	Paul English
JIM MORGAN	Brett Climo

Directed by Bruce Myles
Set and Costume Designer, Judith Cobb
Lighting Designer, Glenn Hughes
Composer, Andrew Pendlebury
Sound Design, David Franzke

CHARACTERS

'The Group':
ALICE FORD, 30s
PAUL ARNOTT, 30s
DEBORAH DEE, late 20s

Elsewhere:
HAROLD HOFFMAN, 60s
NICK FEAST, 30s
JIM MORGAN, 30s

SETTING

Now.

The play has been written to be performed without an interval.

SCENE ONE

Abrupt kill of house lights, simultaneous with a loud hit of music: the Egyptian singer Om Kalsoum.

At once, ALICE *is there, isolated in intense artificial white-blue light.*

It is night.

She is standing still and expressionless, staring ahead.

Music.

Light sweeps away into shadows, leaving just enough to see her face.

She stares ahead.

Louder music.

Figures in yellow traffic-police jackets appear. They carry illuminated traffic wands. They are oblivious to her as they move quickly, efficiently, signalling to one another.

In a sweep of light they are gone.

Light concentrates on ALICE *as the music reaches a pitch.*

Then, at once, she is gone and we are in:

◆ ◆ ◆ ◆ ◆

SCENE TWO

Harold's bedsitter. HAROLD. NICK.

A freezing Melbourne afternoon. HAROLD *is putting on a raincoat, scarf, gloves.* NICK *sits, his sound-recording equipment at his feet.*

HAROLD: There's a little place two blocks away. [*Beat.*] Sophie's Sandwich Spot. [*Beat.*] They know me there. [*Beat.*] It's warm, and the woman, Sophie, on days like today, she'll probably give us a sneaky shot of retsina. It's only a lunch place, but I go there, you see, so I get a sneaky shot of retsina on freezing days. [*Beat.*] She's one of those people who seem to have accepted their life sentence. [*Beat.*] Which in her case is to serve ham rolls and Coca-Cola to the lunch crowd while her *arnaki mi araka* is simmering away in the kitchen. [*Beat.*] She hasn't been discovered by the weekend papers, you see, otherwise she'd be a hero of the peasant cookery movement. So she deals instead with her life sentence. Which was handed down to her at an Australia Day ceremony thirty years ago. An oath of allegiance to Elizabeth the Second and a half-dead eucalypt in a plastic tube. [*Beat.*] 'You are sentenced to give the people what they want, Sophie. White bread. And soft drink.'

Beat.

But they're canny, these women. They can pick you. I sat in there the first time, in Sophie's Sandwich Spot, and had a ham sandwich and a Fanta with the rest of them, but she'd picked me. The next time I went in, she said, 'No ham sandwich. I think you'd like something else.' And I did. It was a plate of what I just said: *arnaki mi araka.* [*Beat.*] Lamb and pea stew, really, but very highly flavoured with dill-weed, and very, very good. Next time I went in, a day like today, half a teacup of retsina.

Beat.

Life's full of little homecomings. Often to places we've never been. Sophie's brother was murdered by the Generals. I said to her: Why do you listen to this dreadful radio station? This dreadful man with his silly views and his lousy advertisements and his awful talkback with people failing to express themselves on subjects about which they know nothing? [*Beat.*] 'It's for the customers', she said. Well bugger the customers. Put on some Theodorakis. Let's not give the people what they've been told to want, let's give them what we know they bloody well need. [*Pause.*] That was by way of asking if you'd like to go and have a coffee. [*Beat.*] Nick?

NICK: No, I mean, I just wish I'd had the tape running.

Beat.

HAROLD: Why?

NICK: It's great, maybe you can tell me again. When I've set up. And I don't mind staying here.

Pause.

HAROLD: Don't you? [*Beat.*] I do. [*Beat.*] Look. That's my bed just there. And that is my wardrobe. My sink is there, my toilet behind that door. If I open that door and sit on my toilet I can see every part of my room.

Pause.

NICK: We'll go out. We'll go to Sophie's.

He picks up his sound equipment. Beat.

HAROLD: Why do you wish you'd had your tape running? I thought you wanted to talk about justice.

NICK: I do.

HAROLD: Then let's go and talk about justice.

NICK: Lead on.

HAROLD: I would. I would lead on. But you have to move to the left of my chair otherwise I can't get to my door. How did you find me?

Beat.

NICK: You're not exactly unknown. [*Beat.*] I drew up a list of names. Chose the ones I wanted to do, delegated the rest, and came hunting. [*Beat.*] In your case I rang a few lawyers. Found one who's seen you around town a bit. And followed the trail. [*Beat.*] It's not as if you've changed your name.

Pause.

HAROLD: Driscoll. The man you spoke to. Tony Driscoll—

NICK: —that's right—

HAROLD: —QC. [*Beat.*] He's got chambers in King Street. I thought he saw me. I thought he saw me but I thought he looked away.

Beat.

NICK: He said you were a bit of an icon.

HAROLD: Did he? It pays to be careful when the Australian Left start talking about icons. They are either being very sentimental, very ironic, or feeling slightly guilty. The Left in this country has icons because it has no victories. All the lost causes have the best monuments.

Beat.

NICK: He only said a bit of an icon.

HAROLD *smiles.*

HAROLD: There's one behind the counter at Sophie's. An actual icon. One of the Greek saints. And whatever happens, you cannot blame the icon. Whatever happens it is never the icon's fault. When the Generals kill your brother, your faith doesn't even flicker. It must be nice. That kind of faith. You don't think I'm a bit of an icon, though. Because I will disappoint you if you do.

Beat.

NICK: No. I don't think you're a bit of an icon.

HAROLD: This list. Who are the others?

NICK: Maggie Hutton.

HAROLD: Maggie Hutton. Mad as a snake.

NICK: Yeh, I'm not doing her. Bob Hill.

HAROLD: Crazy Bobby. Where's he now?

NICK: There's a sort of commune in the Dandenongs.

HAROLD: That'd be right.

NICK: Kind of a mud-brick retirement home. Self-sufficiency, all that. I interviewed him last week. He made me an omelette. Free-range eggs.

HAROLD: Oh, yes.

NICK: Very free-range actually. It took us an hour and a half to find them.

HAROLD: Bob Hill was a brave man. Physically. You see, people will agree to anything in a meeting, but the real test, in those days, was to look a policeman in the eye knowing that he was about to do his duty and break the side of your face. Or to hear two cars drive up outside your house at two a.m. and still answer the front door. Bob would do that. So would Maggie actually. [*Beat.*] I saw her arm broken under a police horse. The same horse that splintered most of Bobby's ribs.

NICK: He told me about that.

HAROLD: The horse made the front page of every newspaper. I think it even had a name.

NICK: Jasper.

HAROLD: That's right. Someone had thrown a bag of marbles and Jasper had a fall. It was touch and go for a while. Not whether the strike would be broken, but whether the courageous police

4

horse would have to be shot. The whole city held its breath. The strike was lost, of course. Eighty-seven men were sacked. But meanwhile the people of Melbourne had pulled together and knitted hundreds of blankets for Jasper. And Brave Jasper pulled through. [*Beat.*] You'd think we would have realised then that the game was up. [*Beat.*] Bob Hill, eh?

NICK: He seemed happy. Happy to talk. It'll be a broadcast in three parts. The ideals. The reality. And a perspective from today. Sowing. Reaping. And whatever that third thing's called. You see there's this great silence on the Left. And I think if we're going to understand this silence, we have to go back and understand the time when there was a bit more noise around.

   Pause.

HAROLD: So we're to talk about the old days, Mad Maggie, Crazy Bobby and me? And who will listen?

NICK: Don't know yet. Radio, it's always hard to judge. You think no one's listening, and then suddenly it turns out everyone was.

HAROLD: It interests you, this sort of thing?

NICK: Well, clearly.

HAROLD: And you'll probably start the program with 'The Internationale'. Played on a scratchy record to convey the feeling of lost ideals.

   NICK *is smiling.*

NICK: It hadn't occurred to me, but it's not a bad thought.

   Pause.

HAROLD: All right. [*Beat.*] But one thing I'd like us to be very clear about, Nick. Because I can't stand arguments in sandwich shops. This is your shout.

◆ ◆ ◆ ◆ ◆

SCENE THREE

ALICE's *flat.* ALICE. PAUL. DEBORAH.

PAUL: I think I was doing it to the wrong people.

DEBORAH: What do you mean?

5

PAUL: I think I was diverting the wrong people onto the freeway. The ones I saw. They didn't look like the ones we were meant to be after.

DEBORAH: How do you know?

PAUL: They didn't look the type.

DEBORAH: The type.

PAUL: Yeh.

DEBORAH: And what type is that? I ask you. Is there a way of identifying people who are on their way to a Stormin' Norman Shwarzkopf lecture? Do they wear badges?

PAUL: They didn't look the type. They looked like people going home.

DEBORAH: They were not people going home. That was the only road into that place. Everyone who was driving up that road was on their way to hear Stormin' Norman deliver a lecture called 'The Keys to Leadership: Guts, Balls and—' what was it?

ALICE: 'Guts and Brains' I think.

PAUL: 'The Key to Leadership: More than Guts'.

DEBORAH: Whatever it was bloody well called, those people were driving up to the carpark to hear Norman talk about his fucking guts. That's what they were doing. I wonder how poor old Stormin' took it?

PAUL: He's probably out there now. Driving 'round Mordialloc with a rocket launcher in a very bad mood.

DEBORAH: We did splendidly. Before the cops arrived, five hundred cars, average two people a car, about a thousand people, were diverted onto the freeway and missed hearing Stormin' Norman. Diverted onto the freeway, I might add, by people they assumed to be traffic police. Perfect: a really nice fuck-up delivered by people in authority. It's got irony, it's got style—

ALICE: —it's got press coverage.

PAUL: I thought we didn't go after that sort of thing.

ALICE: We don't. It just happened.

DEBORAH: What did it say?

PAUL: Now you want to hear your fan mail.

DEBORAH: God your undies must be tight, mate, they're giving me a wedgie. Lighten up.

ALICE: It said that the police are looking for a group of people who posed as traffic officers and diverted an estimated fifteen hundred—

DEBORAH: Yes!

ALICE: —fifteen hundred cars away from General Shwarzkopf's two hundred dollar a ticket leadership lecture.

DEBORAH: Love it. The wand things were great, I liked those.

PAUL: Where did they come from?

ALICE: Girl at the factory, her husband's brother used to be—look, it doesn't matter.

PAUL: I still think I was diverting the wrong people onto the freeway. That venue does share its carpark—

DEBORAH: I think you should write a Letter to the Editor. About these horrible people who spoil the lives of ordinary citizens—

PAUL: All right—

DEBORAH: Actually. There was a group in Seattle. There's a current affairs show, it's TV, but they do talkback. So this group just rang in, again and again saying yes we agree with you, but each time making it a bit more extreme. So that in the end, I can't remember, but in the end they'd kind of forced the presenter into endorsing capital punishment for jaywalkers. It was great. No? We haven't done anything to the AFL yet, and there's Westpac shareholders on the fifteenth, but that's been done to death, hasn't it? [*Beat.*] Who was doing the bomb threat during the Channel Nine News?

PAUL: Lenny.

DEBORAH: Has he done it?

PAUL: Don't know.

DEBORAH: I'd still love to hit Melbourne Grammar somehow.

ALICE: Talkback. Football. Bomb hoaxes. God. We're one step away from hedge-burning and doing naughty things on the Internet.

PAUL: That was actually my next idea. [*Beat.*] Joking, joking. The only funny thing I heard was someone e-mailing bestiality pictures to the Prime Minister's office, but I thought—. Actually hang on, I was going to say that I thought that was just unfair to his secretary, but that's like me saying I diverted the wrong people onto the freeway. [*He smiles.*] I'm becoming soft, aren't I? I'm becoming: Roy.

7

DEBORAH: Oh, please—

PAUL: We sat here, for three hours—

DEBORAH: Don't remind me.

PAUL: Three hours. Before he finally came out with it. That we could, if we tried, if we closed our eyes and really tried, we could levitate Parliament House into the Bay.

DEBORAH: Sad, sad man.

PAUL: Sad? You called him a fucking wanker. To his face.

DEBORAH: And what a face. Does anyone ever see Lucy? She was good value.

PAUL: Bit one-track. You can't use super-glue for everything.

DEBORAH: Or Martin. Was that his name? Martin? Mark?

PAUL: I was talking to a couple of guys at O'Riley's. Ex-Perth mob. They're keen.

ALICE: New guy tonight.

PAUL: Who?

ALICE: Jim Morgan.

   Beat.

PAUL: As in:

ALICE: As in Jim Morgan.

   Beat.

DEBORAH: You're joking.

   Beat.

PAUL: Yeh, she's joking. Are you joking? She's not joking.

ALICE: I'm not.

PAUL: Really? Fuck. I sort of didn't think he actually existed. I thought 'Jim Morgan' was a sort of generic term for shit-hot things.

DEBORAH: The Gippsland blackouts.

PAUL: That was his.

DEBORAH: Did he do the Kakadu bulldozer thing?

ALICE: Apparently.

PAUL: And he's coming here?

ALICE: He likes our stuff.

PAUL: OK. Right. [*Beat.*] Tonight?

8

DEBORAH: What's the matter? Forget your autograph book?

PAUL: Piss off.

DEBORAH: Need to borrow a curling wand?

PAUL: Where'd you meet him?

ALICE: Around.

PAUL: Where?

ALICE: Around.

PAUL: I wonder about you sometimes.

ALICE: You shouldn't.

PAUL: I think you'd really like to be a spy.

ALICE: A spy.

PAUL: Yeh. I reckon if you had your way, you'd rebuild the Berlin Wall and hang around Checkpoint Charlie doing mysterious things.

ALICE: Is that what you reckon?

PAUL: Yeh. A James Bond girl for the twenty-first century.

ALICE: [*to* DEBORAH] You're closest. Hit him.

SCENE FOUR

Harold's bedsitter. HAROLD. NICK.

NICK *is setting up his sound equipment.* HAROLD *watches.*

NICK: I'm sure it'll be fine, but it's happened to me before. You record somewhere for ambient sound and you end up with a tape full of nothing but ambient sound. It wasn't too bad at Sophie's, but it doesn't hurt to check. This won't take a second. [*Beat.*] Here we go.

    He starts the tape.

NICK: [*tape*] Nick Feast, Harold Hoffman, *The Left Profile*. [*Beat.*] Harold, thank you for giving us your time.

HAROLD: [*tape*] Not a problem.

NICK: [*tape*] Tell me where you've been for the last twenty years.

HAROLD: [*tape*] I beg your pardon.

NICK: [*tape*] Twenty years ago you were a prominent radical lawyer. Then you disappeared. Tell me where you've been.

HAROLD: [*tape*] Christ, I— [*Beat.*] I—

Beat.

NICK: [*tape*] Perhaps, then, if you'd tell me about how you live now.

Beat.

HAROLD: [*tape*] I, uh, I live in a room. I—

NICK *switches the tape off.*

NICK: It's fine.

HAROLD: Fine?

NICK: I thought there'd be all this kitchen noise, but it's fine.

HAROLD: All that stammering? I sound like a fool.

NICK: Oh God, I'm not going to use everything. I'll edit it right down. You won't even hear the questions. There's a good two hours of Bob Hill drifting off topic that's got to go, so don't worry. What's your time like this week? Because it'd be great to do the whole thing over a few days, have a kind of continuity to it.

HAROLD: Of course.

NICK: At some point we'll have to talk about why you were disbarred.

HAROLD: I thought we would.

NICK: I mean it can't all be about justice and the death of socialism, can it?

Beat.

HAROLD: I suppose not.

NICK: I'm sorry, I don't mean to be flippant, the point I'm making is this. The way I see it, people who devote their lives to justice, who fight for the kinds of things you fought for, does it matter whether their own lives are pure and noble? Or do we just put them under a harsher light? And when we put them under that harsher light, are we doing it because we can't stand hypocrisy, or are we doing it because we'll do anything to destroy those people who tell us what's wrong with our world? [*Pause.*] Do you see? [*Beat.*] I have a theory. We're never surprised when someone on the Right is shown to be corrupt. It seems logical, their whole philosophy is grab it while you can. But we scream like mad, and we scream, I reckon, with joy, when someone on

10

the Left is sprung for stealing the stationery. It somehow lets us off the hook, you see? I no longer have to think about justice or cruelty or, or whatever, because the people who force me to think about these things are just as petty as me. It's a sort of moral escape hatch. Am I making sense?

Beat.

HAROLD: But I didn't steal the stationery.

NICK: No. [*Beat.*] I know. [*He turns on the tape.*] Nick Feast, Harold Hoffman, *The Left Profile*. [*Beat.*] Tell me what happened.

◆ ◆ ◆ ◆ ◆

SCENE FIVE

ALICE*'s flat.* ALICE. PAUL. DEBORAH. JIM.

JIM: You want to know my favourite? The one I liked the best? [*Beat.*] They've all been good, but the one I liked the best? [*Beat.*] It was the opening of the new museum. [*Beat.*] That was brilliant. [*Beat.*] Absolutely no other word for it. [*Pause.*] I was thinking about it on the way here. [*Beat.*] About how brilliant it was. [*Beat.*] I was actually living near there, so I saw the whole thing being built. One day a big hole in the ground. Suddenly a big building. Trees brought in on trucks. Fairy-lights everywhere. The night it opened I was walking down past there and you've got limos and cops and all the traffic blocked off. Huge. The newspapers, TV, everyone talking about it. It was the only thing anyone was talking about. For days, that's all there was. Brilliant. I wish I'd been there. [*Beat.*] Whose idea was it?

PAUL: Deborah's.

JIM: Yeh? [*Beat.*] Right. [*Beat.*] And, look, I mean it doesn't matter, I'm just curious, but you know, I sort of wondered: whose vomit was it?

PAUL: Ours. It was all our own vomit.

DEBORAH: There were quite a few of us on that gig.

Beat.

JIM: I see.

DEBORAH: So we had access to quite a lot of vomit.

Beat.

JIM: Right.

Beat.

DEBORAH: Essentially it was BYO.

Beat.

JIM: So you just: what?

DEBORAH: Gladbags. You use gladbags. Gladbag, vomit, rubber band.

JIM: Right. [*Beat.*] How did you get in?

DEBORAH: We were members of the public.

PAUL: We posed as members of the public.

DEBORAH: Thank you. We bought tickets. We dressed up. We walked in.

PAUL: With our gladbags.

JIM: OK.

DEBORAH: And along with all the other members of the public, the actual members of the actual public, who, like us, had paid seventy-five dollars for their tickets, we were given vouchers. Two vouchers. One for champagne. One for the souvenir key-ring. So we got our key-rings, and we got our champagne and we stood amongst the throng on the vast and beautiful imported tiles until the trumpets began to play.

PAUL: A fanfare had been specially composed.

DEBORAH: That's right.

PAUL: You could buy the CD.

DEBORAH: Did we?

PAUL: I can't recall.

DEBORAH: And the lights changed, and we all looked up, hundreds of members of the public looking up to the balcony where the dignitaries stood. Men of unimaginable wealth and their women of unimaginable breasts. Famous faces glittering down at us. Young pigs and their tit-models. [*Beat.*] And as the greatest of the dignitaries, the man whose money had built the place, the man who had named the museum restaurant after his laminated wife, as he stepped forward to speak, with his beautiful white

12

cuffs around his beautiful wrists, as the great hall was utterly hushed—

JIM: You threw gladbags full of vomit at them.

Beat.

DEBORAH: We threw gladbags full of vomit at them. After all, they throw vomit at us.

ALICE: I didn't. [*Beat.*] I threw mine into the crowd.

DEBORAH: Yes that was disgusting. Inspired, but really disgusting. This is possibly more information than you wanted, but I tell you: the combination of Givenchy and vomit leaves an unforgettable impression.

JIM: How did you get away?

DEBORAH: How did we get away?

PAUL: I'm trying to remember.

DEBORAH: Did we take the limo?

PAUL: Or the helicopter?

DEBORAH: No, I think we ran like the fucking clappers, would that be it?

PAUL: Quite possibly.

JIM: Nice coverage.

PAUL: It was.

JIM: It's all anyone was talking about. Who threw the vomit at the museum opening? [*Pause.*] I liked that thing with the dogshit at the Stock Exchange too.

DEBORAH: Thank you.

JIM: And your little Easter frolic at St Patrick's Cathedral.

ALICE: That wasn't us.

PAUL: It was a copycat group. It happens.

DEBORAH: Which is fine.

ALICE: Except for the fact that copycats tend to claim responsibility.

DEBORAH: Which we don't.

JIM: Right.

ALICE: The copycats tend to issue manifestos. They tend to want to be interviewed. They tend to want celebrity. We don't. Because we don't exist, Jim. [*Beat.*] There is no group. No office-bearers, no charter, no minutes. No sub-committees, no committees to have sub-committees to. No votes, no resolutions, no

13

amendments. No secretary, no treasurer, no acting deputy president, no chair. There is no constitution, no agreed set of objectives. Statements are never issued because no statements are made. We are not a democracy, we are a glint in the eye. We are the crack in the windscreen, the stone in the shoe: we certainly don't print a newsletter. To the extent that we exist, we exist for one reason: we are here, by and large, to fuck it all up. [*Beat.*] And this. Jim. Is not a meeting.

    Silence.

JIM: Right. [*Beat.*] What're you doing next?

    Silence.

ALICE: Yeh, go on.

DEBORAH: There are some flats in Altona. Used to be public housing. Seven hundred people evicted. Seven hundred people who no longer exist. Everything jooshed-up. The community laundry is now a sushi bar. Auction tomorrow. We go along and we bid. [*To* ALICE] Can you make it?

ALICE: Early shift.

DEBORAH: Dress: neat casual. We arrive separately. We do not stand together, we do not acknowledge each other. We start our bidding when the price gets hot. One of us wins. That person goes inside. Wastes time talking into a pretend mobile phone until everyone outside has gone away. Then sticks their tongue down the real estate agent's throat.

PAUL: That part isn't compulsory.

DEBORAH: It's what I do. Man, woman, doesn't matter. Big tonguey and a bit of a grope, it's the icing on the cake. Then the game's usually up and we're off.

JIM: Right.

DEBORAH: [*to* PAUL] So that's you and me tomorrow, buddy. I'm getting a lift with Rob. Twelve-thirty sharp. [*To* JIM] The whole thing relies on people coming in with ideas. Our numbers go up, our numbers go down, it doesn't matter. As long as it keeps happening, as long we keep chucking little bits of truth at the Great Big Lie. Sorry. Sounds like a manifesto. It's a problem we have. As soon as we spend any time together, we start turning into a Group. And we're not. We are not a Group.

JIM: What are we then?

DEBORAH: We're just Alice and Paul and Deborah and Jim.

>   *Beat.*

PAUL: If those are indeed our actual names.

JIM: Sorry?

DEBORAH: Don't pay any attention to him, his real name is Nincompoop.

◆ ◆ ◆ ◆ ◆

SCENE SIX

Harold's bedsitter. HAROLD. NICK.

NICK *is recording.*

HAROLD: My client was being persecuted. Harassed with technicalities. It's a classic. Because the authorities are squeamish about death squads, they have to use accountants. Crucify the dissident for his tax returns. If he'd been found guilty he would have lost everything. So he asked me to hold his money in trust. And I did. I stepped slightly outside the boundaries and I held his money in trust.

NICK: Money that he'd got from extortion.

HAROLD: Not proved. Never proved.

NICK: All right. Money that was widely believed to have come from extortion in the building industry.

HAROLD: Innuendo is not evidence.

NICK: Then what happened?

>   *Pause.*

HAROLD: You have to understand. I was quoted in the paper, every case that came up, cases I wasn't involved in, the radio would call me. I was on television. Graffiti at the war memorial, asbestos in the staffroom. In, in hindsight I suppose, you could probably say that I was doing less and less work and making more and more comment, and when this came up, this detail about the money, the money I simply held in trust and never touched, it was the excuse the partners needed, it was the excuse

15

they needed to quietly suggest that the times had changed and that I should go. [*Pause.*] But I would not go. I fought it. This new generation of mates-in-suits for whom the word comrade was a quaint affectation, these identical graduates who would tame the Labor jungle into a place of manicured lawns. It was hard to take them seriously because it was hard to tell them apart. But I thought: No, what they rely on is that you will have no courage. What they rely on is that you won't be brave. [*Beat.*] This meeting. When all our meetings involved sandwiches from across the road and wine from someone's cupboard, this meeting at a naked table. [*Beat.*] Where the evidence was produced. That I was knowingly holding money for an extortionist. That I had become an accomplice to a crime. It was a shabby gambit, this group suddenly using the rule book. I wasn't having any of it. If they wanted me out, they would have to do better than this. I would sound the trumpet and unfurl the flag; in seconds my troops would be with me. But this trumpet, I couldn't get a note out of it. Just the faintest little raspberry. Suddenly my flag looked like a handkerchief and I'm afraid that I was quite alone.

    Beat.

NICK: How do you feel about it now? [*Beat.*] Do you still believe that you were wronged? [*Beat.*] Would you say that your, what?, your style?, was out of step with the ambitions of the firm? [*Beat.*] It was the end of your career, Harold, I want to know how you feel about it. [*Beat.*] Did you think your reputation made you untouchable? [*Pause.*] Do you want to stop for a minute? What about a cup of tea?

◆ ◆ ◆ ◆ ◆

SCENE SEVEN

Alice's flat. Night. ALICE. JIM.

JIM: Well they seem like very nice people.

    Pause.

ALICE: What's that supposed to mean?

JIM: That they seem like very nice people. Why? Aren't they?

    Beat.

ALICE: No, you're right. [*Beat.*] They are.

JIM: Good. [*Beat.*] I mean it's good that they're nice people. Nice people are nice to have around. [*Beat.*] World could do with more of them.

ALICE: All right, what are you saying?

JIM: I'm saying nothing.

ALICE: You think they're dregs.

JIM: I didn't say that.

ALICE: Amateur time-wasters.

    Beat.

JIM: That's not a very nice thing to say about your friends.

ALICE: Out with it.

JIM: I merely remarked—

ALICE: Come on—

JIM: —complimented you, in fact—

ALICE: —Jesus—

JIM: —on your choice of friends.

ALICE: Don't jerk me off, sport, say what you're thinking.

    Beat.

JIM: No need. [*Beat.*] You've said it so much better. [*Pause.*] Time-wasters, eh? Ouch. Only question is. Who's time are they wasting?

ALICE: What does that mean?

JIM: I was showing a bunch of people in Darwin once how you blow up a compressor. A quick lesson, nothing much to it, then we're going to go through the fence at the mine-site and do some damage. Six of us. Three of them turn up with tins of paint. I'm thinking: There's been an administrative stuff-up. The graffiti group have come to the wrong meeting. No. These three enemies of the state don't want to blow up the compressors. They want to paint them. They want to paint wildflowers and endangered mammals on mining company equipment. Conquer the forces of global destruction with charmingly bad art. Oh, and maybe, if there's time, lots of Aboriginal dots. [*Beat.*] You think I'm making it up. I'm not. [*Beat.*] Every room you have ever walked

17

into, a group of people, you look around, and ninety-eight per cent of them are actually foetuses. Grown-up, adult foetuses in jackets and jeans. [*Beat.*] True? [*Pause.*] And you think: Ninety-eight per cent of the people in this room, I'm going to have to feed them. Oh, God, not again, will someone please save me from going through all this again, just once can I please just talk to the two per cent?

Beat. ALICE *is smiling.*

Does that feeling make you a bad person? Does that feeling make you a snob? Just to wish that once, once, the things you want to happen can happen, without feeling as if everyone you touch is covered in some dreadful glue. The chit-chat, the book that's been left out so you'll notice it's being read, the kind of coffee they're drinking, the hint of something sweeter later on, the little hard-ons and wide-ons, the details, the details. The library clag of really nice people.

ALICE *is laughing.*

And you think: just once. Please. [*Pause.*] Anyway. I'll call.

ALICE: Not tomorrow, I've got a long shift.

JIM: What do you do?

ALICE: Fish fingers. Fish fingers, frozen peas and party pies.

JIM: Right.

ALICE: I put small boxes of frozen food into larger boxes. And then I seal the box with tape. And then I send it on its way.

JIM: God.

ALICE: What?

JIM: I was trying to remember when I last had a party pie. Nope. It's gone.

ALICE: Tell me—

JIM: The compressor? You cut through the black plastic hose just below the first valve. Air gets into the works and you've completely fucked it up.

Beat.

ALICE: Got it.

◆ ◆ ◆ ◆ ◆

SCENE EIGHT

Street. DEBORAH. PAUL.

She stands. He sits on the ground.

DEBORAH: How do you think they knew?

> *Beat.*

PAUL: I don't know.

> *Pause.*

DEBORAH: But they did. [*Beat.*] They did know.

> *Beat.*

PAUL: They knew all right.

> *Beat.*

DEBORAH: But how?

> *Beat.*

PAUL: Who knows.

> *Pause.*

DEBORAH: We look OK. [*Beat.*] Don't we? You do. [*Beat.*] Do I?

PAUL: You look fine.

DEBORAH: So how did they know?

PAUL: I don't know. [*Beat.*] I am completely in the dark.

> *Pause.*

DEBORAH: It was the guy with the mobile.

> PAUL *laughs.*

What?

PAUL: The guy with the mobile? Deb. It was an auction. Show me the guy who didn't have a mobile. More information please.

DEBORAH: The one with the blonde tips.

PAUL: Ah. OK. Him. [*Beat.*] What about him?

DEBORAH: He looked at me strangely when we got here.

PAUL: Strangely.

DEBORAH: Sort of knowingly.

PAUL: All real estate agents look at you knowingly. They learn it in real estate agent school. It's a look that's meant to say: I know how much money you've really got.

19

DEBORAH: This was different. It was like he knew who I was.

PAUL: You really are getting paranoid, aren't you?

DEBORAH: OK, so when we started bidding, why were two security guards suddenly pulling us out of the crowd?

PAUL: I haven't figured that out yet.

Beat.

DEBORAH: They knew. They knew.

PAUL: We were probably giving off the wrong signals. Like at the airport. How they watch you on a camera and know who to grab for a search. Body language. There are mannerisms. I've often wondered what they are. I've often thought that if you were smuggling something, the clever thing to do would be to look shifty and nervous.

Beat.

DEBORAH: Right.

PAUL: You know. As a tactic.

DEBORAH: So we've got mannerisms, you think? You think there's something about us that screams out: 'We're not the sort of people who could buy a swanky flat'?

PAUL: Does that bother you?

DEBORAH: No. [*Pause.*] A little bit.

PAUL: I see.

DEBORAH: In that I would like to think that I can be a bit more convincing than that.

Beat.

PAUL: Uh-huh.

Pause.

DEBORAH: So what is it? My mannerism?

PAUL: I don't know.

DEBORAH: I know what yours is.

PAUL: What?

DEBORAH: It's the way you stand.

PAUL: How do I stand?

DEBORAH: Like this.

PAUL: I don't stand like that.

20

DEBORAH: You do. Stand up.

He does.

No, now you're trying not to do it. I'll tell you. I'll keep an eye out and tell you when you're doing it.

PAUL: Even if I do stand like that, which I don't, what does it say? If I do this, what does it say?

DEBORAH: No, you haven't got it quite right. It's more like this. [*Beat.*] No, you kind of—

She adjusts his stance, then stands back.

That's it. Fantastic. [*Beat.*] I've taught you to imitate yourself.

PAUL: You do this with your head.

DEBORAH: I don't OK I do why do I do that? I'm always doing it in photographs, it looks like I've cricked my neck.

PAUL: No it doesn't. It looks—

DEBORAH: What?

PAUL: Quizzical?

Beat.

DEBORAH: Quizzical.

PAUL: Or, not quizzical, listening. It looks like you're listening.

DEBORAH: I probably am! [*Beat.*] But looking like you're listening doesn't say: 'I can't really afford a swanky flat'. [*Beat.*] Does it?

PAUL: Why? Do you want to?

DEBORAH: What? Buy a swanky flat?

Beat.

PAUL: Yeh.

DEBORAH: No. Not really.

PAUL: Do you want to get something to eat? Or, oh. Is that breaking a rule?

DEBORAH: What rule?

PAUL: Didn't we agree to a rule about any of us socialising together? The less we know about each other the better?

DEBORAH: I think we also agreed there weren't any rules.

PAUL: We definitely agreed on that.

DEBORAH: So, you know, if we're hungry, and we want to eat, I don't think we need to have a meeting about it.

PAUL *is smiling at her.*

As long as we don't order the same thing we should be fine.

SCENE NINE

Harold's bedsitter. ALICE. HAROLD.

ALICE: It's soup. Carrot soup.
HAROLD: Lovely.
ALICE: Have you got bread?
HAROLD: No.
ALICE: Right.
HAROLD: Sorry.
ALICE: No, that's all right, although, I mean, it would be nice if you got off your fat arse once in a while and bought a couple of rolls. You can afford a couple of rolls, can't you? Can you?
HAROLD: Yes.

She pours soup from a thermos into mugs.

ALICE: I suppose the gas ring's still fucked, is it?
HAROLD: I've asked them twice.
ALICE: You don't ask, you tell. You pay rent, therefore you tell them to do things.
HAROLD: I can't afford to be a nuisance.
ALICE: Oh, please. Of course you can. Bluff them. Threaten them with tenancy laws that don't exist. They're bluffing you. Bluff them back.
HAROLD: It doesn't work in this building, Alice. They throw people out.
ALICE: They do not.
HAROLD: They threw out the poet.
ALICE: No.
HAROLD: Old Brooksie. She nagged them about her toilet and now she's living in a Brotherhood bin.
ALICE: They can't actually do this, you know.
HAROLD: They can. They do. And they did it to Miss Brooks.

22

ALICE: We've got to find you somewhere else.

HAROLD: I'm perfectly fine here.

ALICE: In a place where you're too frightened to ask about a broken gas ring. That poor woman. I only spoke to her once. I thought she was a bit mad.

HAROLD: She was. I mean, it's a ridiculous way to introduce yourself. 'My name is Lizzie Brooks and I'm a poet.' It's the most improbable thing. Like saying you're an astronaut. We know they exist, poets. They must: libraries are full of books full of poems, most of them probably written by poets, but you don't expect to meet one on a flight of Australian stairs. [*Pause. Sipping*] How is your job? [*Beat.*] Good soup.

ALICE: It's OK, isn't it?

> *Beat.*

HAROLD: Be even better with some fuckun bread.

ALICE: Her poems. What were they about?

HAROLD: All out of print. She said her daughter had the first editions for safe keeping, but that her daughter had gone to live in Cape Town with a doctor. So there were no poems left.

> *Beat.*

ALICE: How does it go? 'First they came for the poets and I said nothing...'

HAROLD: She'll be all right. I'll probably see her 'round the place, bailing people up at the GPO. Introducing herself. It's the proper role of the artist in this century in Australia: making unwelcome approaches to disbelieving strangers.

ALICE: You're a cruel man.

HAROLD: What was I meant to do? Nail myself to her door?

ALICE: Yes.

HAROLD: How are your little projects?

ALICE: Fine, Harold, thank you for asking. We're doing auctions again. Fucking up a few fancy auctions. Good fun. You should come along.

HAROLD: Oh yes.

ALICE: You should. Actually you'd be handy on a few things. Scrub you up, get you into a suit. Who'd suspect you of having a paint bomb down your trousers?

HAROLD: You're wasting your time.

Beat.

ALICE: Asking you to come along?

Pause.

HAROLD: Of all the things you could do. Using that brain. But these pranks. It seems a waste.

ALICE: I see it differently.

HAROLD: To choose this life. Packing frozen food all day and doing jokes in the evenings. If you had no choice, if this was all you knew—

ALICE: Choice is the point.

HAROLD: When I think of the people I've known who would have given anything to get out of the factory—

ALICE: I'm not the people you knew.

HAROLD: —anything to leave the drudgery behind. But you.

ALICE: 'Minutes away from a law degree.'

HAROLD: Yes—

ALICE: 'Happily married—'

HAROLD: Well that can't have been true.

ALICE: If I hadn't have chosen this life—

Pause.

HAROLD: Yes?

ALICE: There'd be no carrot soup. No card games. You'd have no one to lecture because we would never have met. [*Beat.*] So cheer up. We did meet. We are friends. There is soup. And I did choose this life.

Beat.

HAROLD: It seems to me that you have also chosen to suffer. That is not a choice I understand. To want to change the world? I understand that. But there are lots of ways of trying to change the world. [*Beat.*] You could— [*Beat.*] I don't know.

ALICE *is laughing.*

ALICE: Go on. I'm dying to find out. Finish my law degree and...? [*Beat.*] Wave signs outside embassies? Organise meetings of concerned residents?

HAROLD: That's not what—

ALICE: Join the Labor Party?

HAROLD: Now you're being silly.

They are smiling.

ALICE: We've been through this before, and you just won't follow the logic. Do you ever watch that television?

HAROLD: Yes and I'm very grateful for it.

ALICE: I'm not looking for thanks—

HAROLD: Oh, too much like a conventional response, was it? I can't turn a trick.

ALICE: And what do you see on that television?

HAROLD: The news. And that rather attractive man on *Law and Order*.

ALICE: Can you at least try to concentrate for a second?

HAROLD: Sorry.

ALICE: You see people asking you to give them money for things you don't need, and this is interrupted by ten minutes of something called Drama or ten minutes of something worse called Comedy, in which other people are using and driving and eating the same things that the first lot are asking you to buy.

HAROLD: Yes, dear.

ALICE: Careful. And why do we submit? Because there is no alternative. So it's off to Dream Land with the Big Lie humming in our ears. This is a nation of sleepwalkers. Changing this country isn't about reasonable argument, it's about voltage. Disturbance. Eruptions of chaos.

Pause.

HAROLD: But you and your friends, you just do jokes.

ALICE: We do something. [*Beat.*] And, you know, some of them aren't so funny. [*Pause.*] Anyway.

Beat.

HAROLD: I think they're funny. They're the reason I watch the news.

Pause.

ALICE: I suppose it's *Law and Order* night, is it?

HAROLD: No. That's tomorrow.

ALICE: What then? The men's swimming finals?

HAROLD: I find that a deeply offensive remark, Alice.

ALICE: Where're the cards?

She finds them and begins to shuffle. They settle for a game.

HAROLD: I had a visitor.

ALICE: Yeh?

HAROLD: I'm being interviewed. For the radio.

ALICE: What about?

HAROLD: Justice I think.

ALICE: Really?

HAROLD: Did you know that I was an icon?

ALICE: I'd heard a rumour.

HAROLD: Apparently I am.

ALICE: They came here?

HAROLD: Tracked me down. I took him to Sophie's.

ALICE: How is Sophie's?

HAROLD: Sophie's is good.

ALICE: I met you at Sophie's.

HAROLD: You did.

ALICE: I thought: Who's this old codger scoffing dolmades at nine o'clock in the morning.

HAROLD: You ate them actually. You actually ate them.

ALICE: I did. It was very rude of me.

HAROLD: No dolmades today. We had coffee and pastries. He paid.

ALICE: And you talked about justice.

HAROLD: I did. Or began to. It was good.

Pause.

ALICE: [*of the cards*] I'm out. OK, that was the warm-up, what are we playing for?

HAROLD: There's some dried chickpeas somewhere, we can play for those.

ALICE: Nah. [*She puts her wallet on the table.*] Let's play for real. My shout.

◆ ◆ ◆ ◆ ◆

26

PLAYBOX presents

CRAZY BRAVE

MICHAEL GURR

CAST

ALICE FORD	**Alison Whyte**
PAUL ARNOTT	**James Wardlaw**
DEBORAH DEE	**Fiona Todd**
HAROLD HOFFMAN	**Bruce Myles**
NICK FEAST	**Paul English**
JIM MORGAN	**Brett Climo**

PRODUCTION

DIRECTOR	**Bruce Myles**
SET AND COSTUME DESIGNER	**Judith Cobb**
LIGHTING DESIGNER	**Glenn Hughes**
COMPOSER	**Andrew Pendlebury**
SOUND DESIGN	**David Franzke**
PRODUCTION MANAGER	**Andrew Barker**
TECHNICAL MANAGER	**Baird McKenna**
STAGE MANAGER	**Fiona de Garis**
ASSISTANT STAGE MANAGER	**Kate Blenheim**
VENUE TECHNICIAN	**Frank Stoffels**
LIGHTING OPERATOR	**David M. Murray**
WARDROBE CO-ORDINATOR	**Felicity Hardy**
WORKSHOP MANAGER	**David Roberts**
SET CONSTRUCTION	**Playbox Workshop Staff**
SCENIC ARTIST	**Sandra Drummond**
WARDROBE SECONDMENT	**Erin Kennedy**
STAGE MANAGEMENT SECONDMENT	**Kerrie Lyons**

The National is proud to sponsor The CUB Malthouse.

As part of the community, National Australia Bank is proud to support The CUB Malthouse, Melbourne's Contemporary Arts Centre. But our support of the community goes even further, with a range of banking products tailored to the needs of every individual and business in the area.

Tailoring banking to your needs.

MICHAEL GURR
PLAYWRIGHT

Michael Gurr's most recent play, *Shark Fin Soup*, premiered at Melbourne Theatre Company in 1998. It was directed by Bruce Myles, designed by Judith Cobb, with lighting by Glenn Hughes and music by Andrew Pendlebury. The same team collaborated on his previous play *Jerusalem*, which was first produced by Playbox in 1996. *Jerusalem* won the Victorian Premier's Literary Award for Drama and four Green Room Awards, including Best Play, before touring to Sydney Theatre Company in 1997, where it won the News South Wales Premier's Literary Award for Drama.

Since 1990, Gurr's plays include *Underwear, Perfume and Crash Helmet* and *Sex Diary of an Infidel* (Playbox); *The Hundred Year Ambush* (Victorian Arts Centre); and *DesireLines* (Melbourne International Festival). He has collaborated on each of these with Myles, Cobb and Hughes. *Sex Diary of an Infidel*

toured nationally and was awarded both the Victorian and NSW Premier's Literary Awards for Drama and eight Green Room Awards, including Best Play. His other theatre writing includes a trio of one-act plays: *A Million Dollars, Test Pilot* and *No Serious Damage*, in which he appeared. His plays *A Pair of Claws, Dead to the World* and *Magnetic North* were first performed by Melbourne Theatre Company where he was Playwright in Residence in 1982. Gurr's plays have been produced Australia-wide and on ABC and BBC radio. He has written screenplays, including *Departure* and *Emmett Stone* and directed for the National Theatre Drama School, Victorian College of the Arts, St Martins and La Mama. He has taught acting Master Classes extensively. Michael Gurr was Artistic Counsel at Playbox for three years, running Theatre in the Raw, the company's program of works-in-progress. In 1995 he traveled to Vietnam as part of an Australian Cultural Delegation.

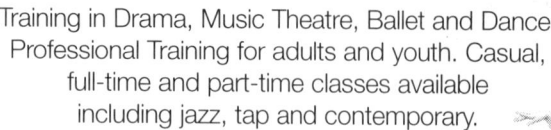

BRUCE MYLES
DIRECTOR

Bruce won the 1996 Green Room Award (Best Ensemble) for the premiere production of Michael Gurr's *Jerusalem* (Playbox). He previously won Green Room Awards (Best Director) for Alex Buzo's *Pacific Union* (Playbox); Gary Day's *Slick;* and *Aftershocks* (MTC). He directed the premiere of Gurr's *Sex Diary of an Infidel* (winning five Green Room Awards including Best Direction and Best Play); premieres of Gurr's *Shark Fin Soup, Underwear, Perfume and Crash Helmet, Desirelines* and *The Hundred Year Ambush;* and the premiere at Playbox of Rodney Hall's *A Return to the Brink*, John Romeril's *Love Suicides* and Louis Nowra's *The Temple;* and Nick Enright's *St James Infirmary*. Bruce played the title roles in *Hamlet, Richard III, Cyrano de Bergerac* and *Amadeus*. Other acting credits include 'Barney' in the premiere of Ray Lawler's *Doll Trilogy; Who's Afraid of Virginia Woolf* (winning a Green Room Award), and the Stephen Sondheim musical *Assassins*. Bruce was director of the award-winning short film *Ruthven* and co-directed the acclaimed feature film *Ground Zero*.

BRETT CLIMO
JIM MORGAN

A well-known television and film actor, this is Brett's first appearance at Playbox. His extensive television credits include: *Eugenie Sandler P.I; Stingers; Close Contact; Blue Heelers; The Man From Snowy River I, II and III; Snowy; GP; Tracks of Glory; Flying Doctors; A Country Practice; Jo Wilson; Vietnam; A Fortunate Life* and *Archer*. Film credits include: *Inner Sanctuary, Blackwater Trail, Body Melt, Dead End Drive In, Going Sane, A Street to Die, Relatives* and *Times Are Changing*. Brett's stage credits include; *Fred* and *Hay Fever* (MTC) and *A Hard God* (Q Theatre).

Victoria University

Proud to be affiliated with Playbox Theatre

For information on courses
Phone +613 9688 4110
www.vu.edu.au
Victoria University,
Melbourne, Australia.

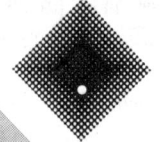

JUDITH COBB
DESIGNER

Judith was most recently at Playbox to design costumes for *Face to Face*. Her other Playbox credits include: set/costume designs for: *A Return to the Brink, Jerusalem, Underwear, Perfume and Crash Helmet, Sex Diary of an Infidel, The Temple, Pacific Union, Waking Eve* and costumes for *The Piccadilly Bushman*. MTC set/costumes designs include *Shark Fin Soup, Closer, St James Infirmary, Macbeth, Top End, The Levine Comedy, Some Night in Julia Creek, Cheapside, Sail, God's Best Country, The Respectable Wedding, A Lie of the Mind, Salonika, Pommies, The Celebrated, Breaking the Silence, Candida, The Christian Brother, Nine Little Australians, The Proposal* and *The Changeling;* and costumes for *I Hate Hamlet, As You Like It* and *Reservoir by Night*. Judith has designed for many other companies ranging from QTC, STC, Adelaide Festival, La Mama and MIFA. Most recent credits are *Queen Kat, Carmel and St Jude* (St Martins), *Hotel Sorrento* (HIT Productions) and *Popcorn* (Letts).

FIONA DE GARIS
STAGE MANAGER

As site supervisor of Perth Festival's *Angel Project*, Fiona's year started with "wing fitting rehearsals" on a CBD carpark roof in forty degree heat. Next, in the icy winds of Wellington's Cuba Mall during the New Zealand Festival 2000, she cleaned the ever smudged windows of the *Urban Dream Capsule*. So it is with some relief that Fiona returns to Melbourne, Playbox, and the world of indoor stage management for *Crazy Brave*. A graduate of both the University of Western Australia and WAPPA, Fiona's production highlights include *The Year of Living Dangerously* (Black Swan), *Omnibus of Dreams* (Festival of Perth), *Lakme* (VSO), *A Return to the Brink* (Playbox), and *Die Fledermaus* (WAO/OA). However, her all-time favourite project was the *Urban Dream Capsule's* appearance at the 1998 Gent Festival, where the crowds were huge and the chocolate plentiful.

PAUL ENGLISH
NICK FEAST

Paul has worked for Playbox in Nick Enright's *Good Works* and Rodney Hall's *A Return to the Brink;* for State Theatre South Australia in *Closer* and *Cabaret;* for the Sydney Theatre Company in *As You Desire Me* and Tom Stoppard's *Arcadia;* and for MTC in more than 20 shows including: *Measure for Measure;* Michael Gurr's *Shark Fin Soup; The Woman in the Window; Much Ado About Nothing; No Going Back; Othello; Racing Demon* and *Europe.* He has a continuing association with Daniel Keene's work through the Keene / Taylor Project and has appeared in *Beneath Heaven, River, What Remains of Dying* and at this year's Sydney Festival in *The Violin* and *A Glass of Twilight.* Paul has worked extensively for ABC Radio in drama and features and has been seen on television in *Possession, The Flying Doctors, Inside Running, Phoenix 2, Blue Heelers* and *SeaChange.*

DAVID FRANZKE
SOUND DESIGN

As a composer for performance, David works predominantly in dance and movement. His recent composer credits include choreographer Cazerine Barry's *Separate at Earth Project* at the North Melbourne Town Hall; The Torch Theatre Company's production of *The Torch,* also at North Melbourne Town Hall; Anna Tregloans *Skin Flick,* a movement-based theatre piece; and Arena Theatre's *Chronic* at the Geelong Performing Arts Centre. His compositions for Playbox include *Elegy, So Wet, Like a Metaphor, Baby X* and *Violet Inc.* (for Inside 2000) *The Sick Room, Thieving Boy / Like Stars In My Hands, Jungfrau* as well as various sound fx / compilations. David is currently working on a creative development with Handspan Visual Theatre and on a maze sound installation for St Martin's Youth Arts Theatre.

GLENN HUGHES
LIGHTING DESIGNER

Glenn started work in theatre in Adelaide in 1973. He travelled to Britain in 1978 where he joined the National Theatre of Great Britain. Upon his return in 1983, he joined the Victorian Arts Centre where he held the positions of Lighting Master (1984-86) and Production Manager (1987-93). He was Production Manager of Queensland Theatre Company from 1995-1997. Glenn's lighting credits include: *A Return to the Brink, Jerusalem, Pacific Union, Underwear Perfume and Crash Helmet, The Temple* and *Sex Diary of an Infidel* for Playbox; *Poppie Nongena, The Hundred Year Ambush, Wish You Were Here, Talley's Folley, A Soldier's Tale, A Portrait of Vincent* (VAC); *Desirelines, 1992 Music Series* (Melbourne International Festival); *St James Infirmary, A Flea in Her Ear, Three Sisters, Shark Fin Soup* (MTC); *Christmas at Turkey Beach, Skylight* (QTC); *Barking Dogs* (MetroArts); *The Conjurers* (La Boite); and *Alice in Wonderland, Rite of Spring* and *Mahler's 10ᵗʰ* (Qld Ballet).

ANDREW PENDLEBURY
COMPOSER

Andrew comes from a classically trained musical family and began studying violin when he was a child, later taking up the guitar. He has played in Melbourne country bands as well as playing guitar and writing for the Australian band, The Sports. He began focussing on instrumental music from 1986 and recorded his first solo album *Between the Horizon and the Dockyard.* His second album *Tigerland* followed in 1987. In 1989, he began performing with Doug de Vries, resulting in two albums, *Karate* and *Trouble and Desire.* Andrew has also worked with Tess McKenna and Dave Steele and performed with Doug de Vries at festivals and venues across Australia. His compositions for theatre include *A Return to the Brink, Jerusalem* and *Shark Fin Soup.* He is currently writing with Chris Wilson's *Crown of Thorns.*

FIONA TODD
DEBORAH DEE

A VCA graduate, Fiona was most recently seen in *So Wet, Baby X* and *Violet Inc.* for the Inside 2000 season. Her other credits include: *Burning Time* for Playbox; *Panacea; Electra Diva* and *Mass* for Arena Theatre Co; *The Blue Hour* for IRRAA and the Adelaide Festival; *Scenes From a Separation, The Grapes of Wrath* and *Pride and Prejudice* (also STC) for MTC; *My Body My Blood* at St Patrick's Cathedral; and *Sharon Lily Screwdriver / Spumante Romantica* at Napier Street Theatre. TV credits include *Janus* and *Blue Heelers*.

JAMES WARDLAW
PAUL ARNOTT

A NIDA graduate, James was most recently seen at Playbox in *So Wet, Baby X* and *Violet Inc.* as part of the Inside 2000 season and last year in Rodney Hall's *A Return to the Brink.* Other credits include *The Visit* at the Carlton Courthouse; *Infectious* for the Melbourne Fringe Festival; *The Taming of the Shrew* in the Botanic Gardens and *My Night With Reg* for EHJ Productions; *The Three Sisters, The Balcony, Lady Windermere's Fan, The Grapes of Wrath* and *Romeo and Juliet* (The MODD Show) for MTC; *The Barretts of Wimpole Street* for QTC; and *The Normal Heart* at Theatreworks. James was a founding member of the Bell Shakespeare Company where his credits include *Romeo and Juliet, Richard III, Hamlet, The Merchant of Venice* and *Much Ado About Nothing.* His television credits include *Stingers, SeaChange, Good Guys Bad Guys, Janus* and *A Country Practice.* Film work includes *Strange Fits of Passion, Redball* and *River Street.*

ALISON WHYTE
ALICE FORD

A VCA graduate, Alison is now a well-established theatre and television actor and was last seen at Playbox in Louis Nowra's *The Language of the Gods*. Other credits include *Searching for Romeo* (State Orchestra of Victoria); *The John Wayne Principle* (STC at Playbox*); Born Yesterday* (receiving a Green Room Award nomination) *Shark Fin Soup, Twelfth Night, St James Infirmary, The Dutch Courtesan, Much Ado About Nothing, The Game of Love and Chance, The Crucible, Morning Sacrifice, Hay Fever, The Taming of the Shrew, Nana, The Heidi Chronicles* and *Present Laughter* (MTC); *Decadence* (winning Green Room Best Actress Award) (Ford O'Connell Productions, Melbourne Comedy Festival, Adelaide Fringe Festival); and *A Midsummer Nights Dream* and *Twelfth Night* (Elston Hocking and Woods). Television credits include *Dogwoman, SeaChange, State Coroner, Good Guys Bad Guys, Frontline, GP* and *The Glynn Nicholas Show.* Her film credits include *Just Do It, Saturday Night, What Goes Around Comes Around* and *The Boatbuilder.* In 1997, Alison won a Silver Logie in the peer voted category.

AND

THE ⓖⒷ MALTHOUSE

PLAYBOX

Playbox is dedicated to the creation, interpretation and promotion of Australian theatre. Since its foundation in 1976, the company has gained a reputation for the presentation of dynamic and progressive drama which reflects our diversity, traditions and place in the contemporary world.

Playbox has pioneered links with the performing arts of the Asia Pacific region and has toured numerous productions throughout this region, as well as introducing various Asian performing arts companies and artists to Australia.

THE ⓖⒷ MALTHOUSE

Located in the heart of Melbourne's arts precinct, **The ⓖⒷ Malthouse** is a lively and versatile venue that has been home to Playbox, its resident theatre company, since opening in 1990. Originally an historic malting house, **The ⓖⒷ Malthouse** offers patrons a choice of two flexible theatres The Merlyn and The Beckett, as well as rehearsal and function rooms, gallery, bar, café and catering facilities.

PATRONS
**Dorothy Hewett, John Romeril,
David Williamson**

BOARD OF DIRECTORS
Paul Gardner (Chairman), **Kate Abrahams,
Douglas Butler, Joan Kirner,
Harold Mitchell, Graham Smorgon,
Haddon Storey, Jarlath Ronayne, John Wood**

Artistic Director **Aubrey Mellor**
General Manager **Jill Smith**

Artistic Associate **Tom Healey**
Artistic Coordinator **Tania Leong**
Literary Manager **Malcolm Robertson**

Finance and Administration Manager
Mario Agostinoni
Assistant to the General Manager Receptionist
Rebecca Walker

Marketing Manager **Damien Hodgkinson**
(Mollison Consulting)
Publicity Manager **Tania Angelini**
Education Officers **Christine Lucas-Pannam,
Margaret Steven**

Production Manager **Andrew Barker** (Playbox)
Production Manager **Michele Preshaw** (Malthouse)
Technical Manager **Baird McKenna** (Playbox)
Head Technician **Frank Stoffels** (Malthouse)
Head Mechanist **Tara La Rosa** (Malthouse)

Venue Manager **Attel Martschinke**
Box Office Manager **Anita Ostojic**
Front of House Manager **Lee Threadgold**
Cafe and Catering Manager **Victoria Gluth**

Workshop Manager **David Roberts**
Workshop **Dave Cotter, Nick Ilton, Ross Murray**

Playbox at The ⓖⒷ Malthouse
113 Sturt Street Southbank Victoria 3006
Box Office **(03) 9685 5111**
Administration **(03) 9685 5100** • Facsimile **(03) 9685 5112**
Email **admin@playbox.com.au** • Web Page **www.playbox.com.au**

Playbox, Affiliated with **VICTORIA UNIVERSITY**

PLAYBOX WRITERS' SUPPORT PROGRAM

Playbox's Writers' Support Program is a vital part of the company's operations.

Each year, hundreds of Australian scripts, including entries for the Playbox/Asialink Playwriting Competition and commissions, come to the company for assessment. All playwrights receive feedback and many plays are guided through several drafts; some receive extensive dramaturgical development and workshopping, some are included in Playbox's Theatre in the Raw series of works in progress and others advance to the stage in the company's subscription season and the Inside season

Playbox co-ordinates with other Australian theatre companies – and developmental agencies such as Stages (WA), Playworks (NSW), Playlab (QLD) and the Australian National Playwrights' Centre (A.N.P.C.) – and co-operates with them in workshops and co-productions.

Playbox is proud of its support of Australian writers and the role it takes as Australia's leading contemporary theatre company. Many companies nationally and internationally are now producing plays that have been developed at Playbox.

Playwrights currently under commission:

Raimondo Cortese	Daniel Keene	Alana Valentine
Anthony Crowley	Tom Petsinis	Evan Watts
Jodi Gallagher	Stephen Sewell	Linden Wilkinson
Dorothy Hewett	Katherine Thomson	

Playwrights currently receiving development support:

Zahim Albakri	Pauline Hosking	Bagryana Popov
Tony Ayres	Margaret Kirby	Therese Radic
Murray Copland	Jo Kukathas	Jema Stellato-Pledger
Kevin Densley	Laura Lattuada	Steven Taylor
Adriano Dino Cugola	Tobsha Learner	Adam May
Christine Gillespie	Tes Lyssiotis	Shaun Charles
Kevin Harrington	Johann McIntyre	
David Hayhow	Tee O'Neill	

Principal sponsors:

ARTS VICTORIA

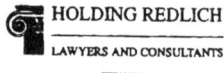

HOLDING REDLICH

LAWYERS AND CONSULTANTS

Annamila Pty. Ltd.

 **BHP**

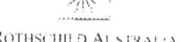

ROTHSCHILD AUSTRALIA

JIM: You guys are fantastic. I'm serious, you're totally adorable. [*Beat.*] But what do you want?

    Pause.

PAUL: I wanna kick that guy's dunny off the hill.

JIM: You don't just want to do jokes? [*Beat.*] Nothing against jokes, jokes are great. [*Beat.*] But. [*Beat.*] There are other things.

◆ ◆ ◆ ◆ ◆

SCENE ELEVEN

Harold's bedsitter. NICK. ALICE.

They stand looking at each other. ALICE *holds a bag of food. Silence.*

ALICE: We should probably organize a divorce.

NICK: Yes, it had crossed my mind. The other day actually. I was having dinner with my parents. And they asked again, about you, again.

    Silence.

And my mother said that I should probably, hang on, how did she put it? I should probably clear up the paperwork. [*Pause.*] They see you in strict nineteenth-century terms.

    Beat.

ALICE: I don't understand.

NICK: You're a bolter. [*Beat.*] You bolted.

    Pause.

ALICE: How are they?

NICK: I beg your pardon?

ALICE: I'm sor—

NICK: How are they? 'How are they?' They're great, Alice, just terrific. My father's nearly finished doing the paving, you remember the paving, you were standing on the unfinished part teasing him about it, bringing him out a beer and teasing him about not ever finishing the paving, and Mum I think, at that point, and she's fine too, by the way, not as cheerful these days

29

I'd say, not the optimist she was, but fine, at that point I think she brought the old camera out and took another photograph because she said you put the kind of smile on my father's face that made him look about twenty-three.

Silence.

Bastard.

Silence.

ALICE: Where is Harold?

NICK: Downstairs. He had to see a man about a gas ring.

ALICE: It would be like this, wouldn't it? It would be something like this. You see, I thought because I wasn't moving in your world—

NICK: What world is that?

ALICE: Yours.

NICK: You'll have to explain.

ALICE: Explain your world?

NICK: Yes. [*Beat.*] I would like to hear my world described to me. From the perspective of one who has left it. [*Beat.*] It would be interesting. [*Beat.*] From a social anthropology point of view. [*Pause.*] Where do you live? [*Pause.*] Then what do you do?

ALICE: I pack fish fingers. In a factory.

NICK: Go on.

Beat.

ALICE: I work different shifts. Sometimes early. Sometimes late.

NICK: Uh-huh.

ALICE: I take the train. Everyone washed and waking up. I go in and I work. I work with women called Hong and Najwa. Najwa has terrible eyesight. She's saving up for decent glasses. We eat lunch together. They talk about their husbands, their boyfriends. Vietnam. Lebanon. [*Pause.*] And then I get back on the train and go home. [*Beat.*] That's what I do.

Beat.

NICK: Bullshit. [*Beat.*] Sorry. Sorry Hong, sorry Najwa, but that's just bullshit. What do you do?

Affiliated with **VICTORIA UNIVERSITY**

AND THE ⓖⓑ MALTHOUSE

would like to **THANK**

GOVERNMENT

ARTS VICTORIA

EDUCATION PROGRAM

eat well
live well

THE AGE
Young Critics
Award

PRINCIPAL SPONSOR

MEDIA & MARKETING

ACP

PRINCIPAL SPONSOR

Bulletin
IN ASSOCIATION WITH

VOLVO

Seize

THE AGE

BORNIAK & CANNY

CORPORATE BRAND
MANAGERS

SPICERS PAPER

SUPPLIER OF
PREMIUM PRINTING PAPER

CPR

MARKETING
STRATEGISTS

ACNielsen

MARKET
RESEARCHERS

 MOLLISON

COMPLETE
MARKETING SERVICES

BRIDE

---

austereo
AUSTEREO PTY LTD

TRAVEL & ACCOMODATION

QANTAS

OFFICIAL AIRLINE
PRINCIPAL SPONSOR

ACCOMMODATION FOR
VISITING ARTISTS

Hotel Sofitel

CORPORATE SPONSORS

COMPAQ

SUPPLIER OF
COMPUTER HARDWARE

oit

WEBSITE DESIGNERS

CORPORATE SPONSORS

THE MYER WEST GROUP

ⓖⓑ

National
Australia Bank

 **POST**
International Services

 **RACV**

GREY

 M P

Arthur Robinson & Hedderwicks

BYTE GRASS

TRESS COCHS & MADDOX

When you've got the tradition, the pride and the spirit it shows in everything you do.

SCENE TEN

Paul's house. PAUL. DEBORAH. JIM.

PAUL: It's not as good as their last one.

JIM: You don't think so.

PAUL: Nowhere near it. [*Beat.*] The last one was fantastic. They recorded it over three days. You can hear that urgency in the music. It feels urgent. But this one? They used a synthesiser, for Christ's sake.

JIM: And you have a problem with that?

PAUL: Yes. [*Beat.*] Yes I do. [*Beat.*] The way I see it, if you've got the time and the money to be mucking around with synthesisers, you've lost your whole reason for being. [*Beat.*] I'm quite firm about this. Their first album was brilliant. This one is a load of shit.

> *Pause.*

JIM: What do you mean their first album?

PAUL: The one before this.

JIM: You've got it wrong. They've put out three.

> *Beat.*

PAUL: No they haven't.

JIM: Sorry. But they have. What you think of as their first album is actually their second, Paul.

PAUL: That's not possible—. [*Beat.*] I mean, I'm a fan, I'd know if there were three albums.

JIM: Their first album was a recording of a live performance. It was only put out on cassette. It was called 'Professor Chimpanzee'. It was mind-blowingly good. [*Beat.*] I'll lend it to you.

PAUL: Thanks.

DEBORAH: Where's Alice?

PAUL: She'll be along later.

JIM: I'm not surprised the auction was a bit of a fizzer. Those guys are so cunning, they're genetically enhanced with rat spoof. Sort of the wrong enemy anyway, isn't it, the try-hard sons of free enterprise?

27

DEBORAH: What do you mean?

JIM: Why pick on the shop-keeping classes? They're eating the same bowl of shit for breakfast as everyone else. [*Beat.*] Why waste our time doing capitalism a favour? Pointing out its faults so it can adjust its face. The greatest allies it has are decent people offering it helpful suggestions. And capitalism is not even the enemy. It barely even bloody exists. A handful of global corporates, that's our lot. We don't need conspiracy theories anymore, the facts of life are all that any crazy bastard could want. 'For the Spirit of Greed is alive in the world, its tongue seduces and its teeth bite down. Trespass and victory in the blink of an eye and the mind and the mouth are one.' So it is written, or should be.

Beat.

Why does the world lose a dozen more languages every year? So that faceless CEOs and their loyal Aussie dogs can build their dunnies a little further up the hill? And if it must be changed, and we agree it must be changed, who will be the ones to do it? [*Beat.*] 'The struggle between greed and justice is an everlasting battle of strategy.' I used to believe that. Above all else it was an article of faith. Until slowly it dawned that the war had been lost. The conscientious citizens had never stood a chance. History was over. I was living in an archive. It was time to start again. [*Pause.*] How serious are you?

DEBORAH: On a scale of one to ten? I don't know about Paul, but I'm probably about a nine.

PAUL: I'm about seven and a half I think and that's just because I don't want to live without television.

DEBORAH: Or toothpaste. I don't think they have toothpaste at Year Zero, do they?

PAUL: Or Tim Tams.

DEBORAH: I told you that in confidence. And you're doing it, by the way.

PAUL: What?

DEBORAH: Standing in your mannerism.

PAUL: I wasn't going to mention the whole neck thing—

Pause.

ALICE: I'm talking to a journalist.

NICK: No you're not.

ALICE: What, you're not doing this radio—?

NICK: I'm your husband.

Pause.

ALICE: I do some political stuff.

NICK: Yes.

ALICE: I don't want to go into details, it's just stuff.

NICK: Stuff.

ALICE: Yes.

Pause.

NICK: OK. [*Beat.*] So, uh, don't tell me what you do. Tell me, though, instead, why you do it. What's your, you know, what's your: aim?

Beat.

ALICE: We want to do something to help destroy the society that we live in.

NICK: Gosh.

ALICE: Yep.

NICK: And how do you hope to do that? [*Pause.*] We. So you're in some group.

Beat.

ALICE: I just want to establish something. [*Beat.*] That you weren't looking for me. Through Harold. That you knew we were friends and you're interviewing him so—

NICK: I stopped searching for you exactly one month after you left. [*Beat.*] The police said: No Suspicious Circumstances. She's just packed up her life and gone. My father wanted a private detective. He thought you might have had some kind of mental disease. To have simply walked away. But I look at you now. And you're not crazy. He said maybe you were, but you're not. He said: You probably couldn't have held her, Nick, she's three parts flamenco.

Silence.

You see, I thought my moment of greatest terror had come and gone. I thought: Well, I've had my moment. That won't happen again.

Beat.

ALICE: What do mean terror?

NICK: When I asked you to be waiting on the pontoon by the bridge at nine o'clock. A surprise, I said. Did you know that I hired and cancelled a band three times before I finally settled on no music, no waiters, just the man who drove the boat and a ton of flowers on board? Well, of course you didn't know that, what a stupid thing to ask. [*Beat.*] Then there was the question of what kind of flowers. It was the wrong season for everything. Then: snap. I thought of it. Not flowers. Leaves. Garlands of leaves. That's it. The boat should look like a floating garden.

Pause.

So we were hiding 'round the bend. The boat driver and me. He was tremendously excited, he thought his boat looked fantastic. Actually, sorry, his exact words?: 'shit hot'. [*Beat.*] So at nine p.m., right on the button, we come chugging 'round the bend. And that was my moment of terror. No one on the pontoon, you see. He asked me if I wanted him to turn around and come back again in a minute. Perhaps you were running late. Was I sure this was the right pontoon? So we did that. We turned the floating garden around, went back around the bend, turned around again, and came back. [*Beat.*] It took forever. But this time you were there. [*Pause.*] And we went up and down the river for hours, you and I. The whole city, lit up, all ours, all belonging to us. And our boatman was professional to a tee, wasn't he? He kept his eyes on the river, never looked at us once. [*Beat.*] That was the world we moved in. That was the world you left. [*Beat.*] The world you say you want to destroy. [*Beat.*] If I've understood you correctly.

Pause.

When you weren't there I thought everything was lost. [*Pause.*] Once you've succeeded, I want to know this, once you've succeeded in destroying this world, what exactly have you got in mind for us? You must have a plan. A blueprint. A charter of principles for the new world we will all inhabit. Perhaps you've got a pamphlet about it. Something I could take home and read at my leisure.

Pause.

ALICE: There are one hundred and thirty-four varieties of deodorant in Safeway, Nick. I counted them: one hundred and thirty-four. [*Beat.*] I don't believe in blueprints. There is no charter of principles. The mistake is thinking that there is something definitive. Some definitive destination, a place you actually arrive at, or if there is, that it's remotely likely we'll get there in anything like the next million years. Sometimes I think it's all down to the wrong monkey. [*Beat.*] The wrong monkey getting pushed off the branch. You know? Two monkeys in a tree. One finishes eating his berries. Very nice, he thinks. I'd like some more. Looks at the other monkey. Hang on, I'll take his. I'll just steal his berries and push him off the branch. So he does. [*Beat.*] And that was it. All the genetic material for goodness was shattered on a rock in about four billion BC. And now there's us: all descended from the wrong fucking monkey and picking our arse in Las Vegas.

Beat.

The point is change. That's all there is. And nothing burns down by itself. I say leave the bright new world to some future time when people might know what they want. I mean, would you buy Utopia from me? [*Beat.*] Christ, I wouldn't. [*Beat.*] The way I see it, our duty is lighting fires. Getting out of this unbelievable rut. You know, when '99 ticked over into 2000, you could just about hear it, this great worldwide Nothing. Nothing happened. Not even some gorgeous, crazy Jew going apeshit at the Wailing Wall. Nothing. Just more rut. Rut forever. Rut forever and rut without end amen.

Beat.

That's our faith. A world of window-dressing. Some sad bastard saying if only we were nice to the forests. Really? Capitalism

33

will save just enough forests to keep us satisfied. Satisfied that our fridge magnets have achieved something. Just enough of the world kept breathing to put a gloss of civilisation on our happy-barren lives. One forest. One cute species. One very slightly progressive government every now and then. God it makes my skin itch. This life of anaesthetic. [*Beat.*] And out on the edges of it are the tired people, the exhausted people, the people we pay a pittance to mop up the vomit, to keep the ugly out of sight, the homeless away from the shopping centres, and the crazy fully doped. These people beg, they beg for a dollar more. Three more beds, please, in our piss-stinking hostel, please can we have a translator in the travelling outback courtroom so the prisoner will know what's going on? And please, if you're still listening: a mini-bus to drive our mad people to the You-Yangs, where with any fucking luck they'll all fall down a hole? Please?

Beat.

You can't even say the word socialism in this country. You can't even say justice. Justice in this country is when no one is being actively nasty to you. Justice is when you're allowed to join in the Great National Sleep. I mean, is that a distinction? Is that a measure of pride? To live in a sorry, grasping world with a cheerful face? Should we all be happy with that? Should we be impressed? Is it time to pipe 'The Internationale' over the sound system at K-Mart? [*Beat.*] What an ambitionless lot we are. [*Beat.*] My tram got stuck behind the Anzac Day march and I thought: what happened? You people fought Nazis. What happened? Did you just come home and go to sleep?

Silence.

You see it's this. [*Beat.*] All I want to do is speed up human evolution a little bit. I want to light some fires. I want to burn us out of the undergrowth and onto the plain. [*Beat.*] That's all.

Silence.

NICK: Where do you live?

Pause.

34

ALICE: That's food. He does this hopeless act with cooking. [*Beat.*] Get him to tell you the story about the woman and the loaf of bread. He thinks of it as his finest moment. [*Beat.*] He's absolutely over the moon that someone's interested.

◆ ◆ ◆ ◆ ◆

SCENE TWELVE

Paul's house. PAUL. JIM. DEBORAH.

JIM *is reading a piece of paper.*

JIM: '—and four parts sugar. Heat over a low flame until it melts, stirring well. Pour into container and, before it solidifies, embed a few matches into the mixture to act as fuses. One pound will fill up a whole city block with thick, white smoke.' [*Beat.*] One pound. It's an American recipe. What's that in kilos?
PAUL: God it's simple.
JIM: Utterly.
DEBORAH: A whole city block.
JIM: Yep.
DEBORAH: Lordy Mumma. And it's only smoke.
JIM: Yep.
DEBORAH: Show me the delegate list.

JIM *hands her the list.*

PAUL: I like this because it's saying: This could have been an actual bomb. It's only a smoke bomb, but it could have been an actual bomb. That's what I like about it. It really announces a presence. I mean, God we'll have to be careful.
JIM: Aren't you usually?
PAUL: Sure, but this is like, if we got done for it, you wouldn't just be looking for a magistrate with a sense of humour. You'd be looking for a mighty fine lawyer.
DEBORAH: This a sensational list. The Crown Royalty of Australian business.
JIM: It's not bad is it?

35

DEBORAH: 'Goodwill Australia brings together the most successful businesspeople in the country in a unique and ground-breaking...' bullshitbullshitbullshit— '... to meet with and listen to representatives of the most underprivileged sections of Australian society. Goodwill Australia is a genuine attempt by Australian business to meet its social obligations and find solutions based not on handouts but on goodwill.' The marketing department have told them to be seen with some photogenic losers. Touching, isn't it?

JIM: And this is just the kick-off. After this, every capital city, every regional town.

PAUL: How do they pick them?

DEBORAH: The losers? Easy. The least offensive single mother. The tidiest homeless kid. The quietest Koori. 'Each table will have at least one Goodwill Delegate seated with them.'

JIM: Be interesting to see who gets to the exits first.

PAUL: It's not actually a worry that this event has got, you know, a whole lot of support, is it? Shut up, Paul.

JIM: It's air freshener, mate. Air freshener over a frying turd.

DEBORAH: Three major banks, all the big mining companies, that sleaze who owns half the football. It's one with the lot.

PAUL: This is going to need very careful planning. These people might be playing Citizen Nice Guy, but a million to one there'll be some serious security and I have this irrational fear of jail.

JIM: [of a rolled-up map] Floor plan.

PAUL: Good.

JIM: All doors marked, including Plan B which is through the kitchens and carpark.

PAUL: Great.

JIM: Master key for external locks to security exits. When will these people ever learn?

PAUL: How'd you get this stuff? Sorry.

JIM: We go in, we detonate, we get out and we meet at the pub in a week.

DEBORAH: I can't wait for Alice to hear about this, it's exactly the kind of thing—

JIM: She knows, she loves it, this is what we thought for a breakdown of who's responsible for what.

He hands them a sheet of paper each.

PAUL: God this is going to be so unpopular.

JIM: You're right. People will hate you. You should prepare to be hated. Little secret, it's actually the best part.

◆ ◆ ◆ ◆ ◆

SCENE THIRTEEN

Harold's bedsitter. HAROLD. NICK.

HAROLD *is eating.*

NICK: I followed her. [*Beat.*] Whether she knew or not, I don't know. [*Beat.*] But I had to see where she lived. [*Beat.*] You see? [*Beat.*] I mean I'm understandably curious. [*Beat.*] Have you visited her there?

Beat.

HAROLD: Yes.

NICK: What's it like? You see I have this picture. It frightens me. Nothing on the walls. Hardly even a bed.

HAROLD: It's nice. Simple. There are books. A little stereo. The things people have. No television. She gave that to me.

Pause.

NICK: And is she alone there?

HAROLD: She lives alone, yes.

Beat.

NICK: You see I imagined nothing on the walls, nothing in the cupboards.

HAROLD: No. There are some pictures. And she cooks.

NICK: Yes. [*Pause.*] It's a terrible building though. Rotten. Right on that bloody road. Fucking trucks going past. [*Pause.*] Do you think I'm crazy? For following her? [*Beat.*] I think she was. For vanishing. [*Pause.*] Of course I was going to follow her. [*Beat.*] I watched her go inside and then I caught a bus out of there. Tried to catch a bus. They go in these ridiculous directions. City via North-West Woop-Woop.

Beat.

HAROLD: I don't think you're crazy.

NICK: No, well, I don't think I am either.

HAROLD: Love. It's the great non-sequitur. The non-answer to every question.

NICK: Yeh, pretty good, you could probably say that later on tape if you wanted to.

HAROLD: I'm sorry?

NICK: No, OK, look, you're right, I should probably be getting on with this. I thought it might be a good idea to talk about the best thing that ever happened. You know? Everyone's got a horror story, everyone loves pessimism, but what about the victories? I listened back to all the stuff I got from Bob Hill and it's one long list of failure. All the things that nearly happened. Great long sagas about how the Left tore itself apart. Not a single note in a major key. And I thought: Is this what happens? Is this what happens to the revolutionary spirit in Australia? It becomes nostalgic for defeat? [*Pause.*] Bob Hill actually achieved things. He actually has cause for pride. But you wouldn't know it from listening to him. This endless symphony of regret. The same tune we always hear from the Left, with half the orchestra walking offstage because it got too tired or too comfortable or because it just thought that defeat would make a better anecdote. [*Beat.*] And Maggie Hutton? Mad Maggie? I listened to some of the stuff they've taped of her. And her very first words. Can you guess what they were? [*Beat.*] 'My one regret is that we were too polite. We sat down and talked with the enemies of progress, when really we should have just shot them.'

Beat.

HAROLD: Maggie fucked a lot of Irishmen. [*Beat.*] So did I, now I mention it.

NICK: [*turns on tape*] Nick Feast, Harold Hoffman, *The Left Profile*.

HAROLD: But no one ever thought of guns. The best thing any radical can do is learn the rule book. Because the enemies of progress will always break the rules. Fill your head with legal detail and you've got 'em by the balls, Now. No more pessimism? No more nostalgia for defeat? Away with regrets and bring on the tales of victory? Good. [*Beat.*] I'll tell you a story. A true story. It's a story about a woman and a loaf of bread.

◆ ◆ ◆ ◆ ◆

SCENE FOURTEEN

Alice's flat. ALICE. PAUL. DEBORAH. JIM.

ALICE *is kneeling on the floor with a ground plan. There is muffled but persistent techno music coming from the upstairs flat.*

ALICE: No. No. You're not there. You're here. Jesus. Look. Everyone give me something. [*She takes off a ring. Puts it on the ground plan.*] Here. I'll be the ring. Deborah.

DEBORAH: I'm a twenty-cent coin.

PAUL: I'm a dollar.

ALICE: Jim.

JIM: Door key.

ALICE *arranges the objects on the map.*

ALICE: Right. So let's start again. I start here. Twenty cents there. Dollar at this door. And where are you?

JIM: Opposite door.

ALICE: Door key at opposite door. [*Beat.*] Right. [*Beat.*] Then what happens?

JIM: Then we follow the plan.

ALICE: I know we follow the plan, but we should go through the plan. That's why we're here. Is to go through the plan.

DEBORAH: Are you OK?

ALICE: Of course I'm fucking OK, isn't wanting to go through the plan a fucking OK thing to do? [*At the ceiling referring to the music*] Shut up! [*Pause.*] Look. Would someone do me a favour? It is impossible to think, and I've been up twice today already. He's Ben, she's Kimmy, they won't hit you or anything.

PAUL: I'm on it.

But JIM *has gone. Pause. They wait.* ALICE *sits with her head in her hands, then gazes up.*

ALICE: They're new. My quiet Timorese gay boy moved out.

Beat. The music stops.

[*Sighing*] OK. Sorry for the shouting. How are you both?

DEBORAH: Good.

PAUL: Yeh.

Pause.

DEBORAH: This is good.

ALICE: It's fantastic.

PAUL: There are a couple of—

ALICE: Scary. But you know, what's the point of continuing if we're not going to get real.

Beat.

PAUL: There's a couple of things that worry me a—

JIM *returns.*

ALICE: Thank you. All right. I'm not running this. Door key. You're running this. What's next?

JIM: Well, the map's just the map. We can all have a look at the map. And we've got a list of times of when we have to be where we have to be. So, I guess we just do it.

Beat.

PAUL: When do we make the smoke bombs?

JIM: Done.

PAUL: All of them?

JIM: Yep.

PAUL: Oh.

JIM: Sorry.

DEBORAH: Boys boys boys.

PAUL: What, didn't you want to help make them?

DEBORAH: No, actually. I have no interest in standing over a stove stirring a whole lot of toxic chemicals together.

JIM: Not toxic.

PAUL: So where are they? I mean, we need to see how to light them.

ALICE: Kitchen. They just look like birthday cakes made of soap. All you do is light the candles.

Beat.

40

PAUL: Right. [*Beat.*] So how do we put them into place?

JIM: Doing it later. Easy job. [*He shows an ID.*] Jim Morgan. Security for Goodwill Australia.

> *The techno music from upstairs kicks in again, a little louder than before.*

ALICE: OK. If everything's fine and we all know what we're doing—

PAUL: I do have a couple of questions.

ALICE: We may be one smoke bomb short. I may go upstairs and use one tonight.

PAUL: Sorry, can I—?

ALICE: Guys. I'm out of here. I'm going to lose a week's wages on the pokies and then get a good night's sleep. Let yourselves out, we'll meet on the day. It'll be great.

> *She has kissed* DEBORAH *and* PAUL *during this and now leaves. Beat. The upstairs music moves up a notch.* JIM *leaves. The upstairs music moves up another notch.* PAUL *and* DEBORAH *look at each other.*

◆ ◆ ◆ ◆ ◆

SCENE FIFTEEN

Harold's bedsitter. HAROLD. ALICE.

She carries half a dozen books.

ALICE: These are yours.

HAROLD: Are they?

ALICE: Yes. You lent them to me. I've read them. I'm bringing them back.

> *Silence.*

So here they are.

> *Beat. She puts the books down.*

HAROLD: Thank you.

> *Pause.*

41

ALICE: Sorry. I didn't bring anything. I haven't had time. Work. Other things. You know Najwa?

HAROLD: At the factory.

ALICE: She broke her arm.

HAROLD: At the factory?

ALICE: No, actually, no, it was strange. She came to work and her arm was broken. She had it in a sling, but it was broken so, you know, there went the rest of the day.

HAROLD: You took her to hospital.

ALICE: Yes.

Silence.

HAROLD: Is she all right?

ALICE: Well, yes. [*Beat.*] She is. She can't really work, of course, but the doctors were fantastic. Everyone thought it was her husband. She wears that sort of half-veil, so everyone assumed her husband had done it, but in fact she fell down the stairs at her flats, she's blind as anything and won't buy daggy glasses, you see. [*Beat.*] Are the interviews going well?

HAROLD: Yes.

ALICE: What's it like, talking about yourself like that?

HAROLD: I feel I've been peering in for a very long time. You know? Nose pressed to the glass, then hurrying on. But I rang someone. Tony Driscoll. Do you know who I mean? [*Beat.*] Years ago he was a young lawyer. Now he seems to want to meet me for lunch. I'm going to be on the radio, you see. So now I'm allowed to be seen. His favourite restaurant is in a lane up near Parliament.

Beat.

ALICE: That sounds nice. [*Beat.*] You're being invited back in. [*Beat.*] Sounds like a long way from Sophie's. [*Beat.*] Sounds like a long way from everything. [*Beat.*] She'll miss you. [*Beat.*] She'll miss that toast you do to the death of the men who killed her brother in the furnace of a cellar in Athens. A teacup of retsina to the end of fear and to man's ascending soul. I thought that was a call to arms. I was wrong. It's a lullaby. A lullaby. I wish I could tell you what it feels to be completely awake.

Silence.

HAROLD: Where do you think you are? [*Beat.*] All over the world there are people who are fighting for their lives. Women and men who wake up each morning, if they wake up each morning, to the possibility of rape, the possibility of a beating from the lucky bullies who rule them, death if they're fortunate, or maybe just to disappear. [*Beat.*] People literally fighting for their lives. And here? This country? What on earth are you fighting for? Nothing as real as blood, nothing you can even point at. Not a valley you're trying to take, not a crop you should be paid for or a prisoner you want released.

Beat.

Every generation discovers this for themselves. That in this country you are fighting an invisible force. And that's why we lose them, in their thousands we lose them, good kids with righteous hearts, each new battalion coming up, over the top of the trench to fight: what? The battle for a nation's soul? I ask you. [*Beat.*] You are wrestling with a column of smoke. And that's all we can tell our troops. At best you'll be the entertainment. That rage you feel? It will look like slapstick on the evening news. That gesture you make? A fart for a laugh. [*Beat.*] You are fighting every man in every park with every dog. You are fighting every family at every meal. You're telling every mother at Christmas that she's the damn-fool victim of a shit-brown lie.

Pause.

And there's something else we have to say to our troops, as they defect in their thousands. We have to say we can't blame them. We wished for a Bastille, we wished for Generals, we wished for the thing that would make it all clear. But they don't go down to gunfire, our battalions. They don't go down to tanks. They go down instead to the chloroform of sunlight. And who can blame them. You're fighting laughing gas. The Australian Revolution? Dead of happiness. And how does it go, this country's anthem of rebellion? How does it go, the great galvanising tune? 'The people are happy and it all seems wrong.' [*Beat.*] The cruelty of happiness in a stinking world.

43

Silence.

Tony might get a few old friends together. I mentioned I was up for eviction. That the clock was ticking on this building. He just laughed. There are spare rooms all over the city, he said, if you only know where to look. Apparently lunch went out of fashion in the nineties and now it's back in. *[Beat.]* Life's full of little homecomings. I'd like a few lunches with a few old friends.

ALICE: What's happened about the gas ring?

HAROLD: Nick fixed it. The problem with people, Alice, is that we can't live in their absence. An idea can be magnificent, but it doesn't give off much warmth. *[Pause.]* I didn't want this exile. And the feeling that it might be over—it's my floating garden coming 'round the bend.

Silence.

ALICE: I'm happy for you. But it wasn't a floating garden. It was a prison ship.

◆ ◆ ◆ ◆ ◆

SCENE SIXTEEN

Split scene.

Harold's bedsitter. HAROLD. NICK.

ALICE'*s flat.* ALICE. JIM. *She stands watching him as he keys words and figures into a pocket organizer.*

A pub. PAUL *stands with two drinks. He hands one to* DEBORAH.

NICK: I forced the kitchen window. Climbed in over the sink. It's so embarrassingly easy I wonder why more people don't do it. *[Pause.]* I had to see for myself. *[Beat.]* It's unrecognisable. *[Beat.]* I mean, I wouldn't have recognised her from this place. Not the clothes, not the music she's got. For a minute I wondered whether I'd broken into the right flat. *[Beat.]* What I'm actually saying is that there was nothing of us. I have no presence there. I have been: expunged is the word, I think. Her kitchen is a bomb factory. *[Beat.]* Were you aware of that?

44

[*Beat.*] She cooks all right, I saw the recipes. One for smoke bombs, she'd already made those. Lined up on the bench like a cake shop. And one for something else. A whole list of things I didn't understand. I copied it down. Do you understand this?

NICK *passes* HAROLD *a scrap of paper.*

You don't recognise anything. [*Beat.*] It sounds dangerous.

PAUL: Are you scared?

DEBORAH: Are you?

PAUL: Yes.

DEBORAH: I think it's because we're doing it at night.

PAUL: That's probably it.

He drinks.

DEBORAH: Although most of the other things have been at night.

Beat.

PAUL: Except the Stock Exchange.

DEBORAH: Yes. That was during the day. [*Beat.*] Early morning actually.

JIM: Do you know about tennis-ball bombs? Very easy. So easy it's embarrassing.

NICK: How would we find out? Who would we ask?

HAROLD: I don't know.

JIM: Do you know what you can do with a packet of fertiliser, a wad of newspaper, some cotton wool and diesel fuel?

PAUL: How do you think things are going?

DEBORAH: With the group?

PAUL: Generally.

DEBORAH: Can I make a confession?

PAUL: Please.

DEBORAH: I voted at the last election.

PAUL: Really?

DEBORAH: Yes. I enrolled. And then I voted.

PAUL: Wow.

DEBORAH: So that must say something.

PAUL: Well, yes.

DEBORAH *drinks.*

45

NICK: Are you going somewhere? You've taken everything off the walls.

HAROLD: I'm moving. Friends have helped me find a better place.

NICK: What should I do?

HAROLD: About this?

NICK: Yes.

HAROLD: I don't know. Why don't you talk to her?

NICK: Why don't you?

JIM: Cracking an ATM? Lock-picking for beginners? Strobing-out a security camera?

NICK: There was a ground plan as well. Of Riverside. The function centre. Air-conditioning ducts. Red dots on all the entrances and exits. It's this Goodwill Australia thing. What do you think they're doing?

JIM: The ticket machine codes?

HAROLD: On the evidence you've given me so far, I'd say they were planning to throw in a smoke bomb.

NICK: You don't think we should do something about it.

JIM: The gas meter trick?

HAROLD: The telephone number for the police is not a secret, Nick. You do whatever you feel you must. And be sure to mention your burglary.

JIM: How about petrol and styrofoam? You'll pick it up in no time.

PAUL: What do you think of Jim?

DEBORAH: I think he's great for this sort of thing.

> PAUL *drinks.*

PAUL: What do you think of Alice?

DEBORAH: I've always wanted to have her 'round for dinner, but I get the feeling she'd find the idea suffocating.

> DEBORAH *drinks.*

NICK: But this other thing. This list of ingredients. What's that? What if—?

HAROLD: What if what?

JIM: All we have to remember is that nothing is impossible.

HAROLD: What if what.

JIM: Absolutely nothing.

PAUL: So you feel you might want to move on?

DEBORAH: I'd miss the secrecy.

PAUL: And what do you think of me?

DEBORAH: You turn me on. I've wanted to get into your pants since the first moment I saw you.

PAUL: Just my pants?

DEBORAH: It's a metaphor. Your pants are a metaphor for everything about you.

NICK: There is something else actually. The last session. I listened back to it and there's this buzz I can't get rid of. I'm going to have to ask you to tell me that story again.

HAROLD: We'd better get started then.

JIM: Feeling brave? How about changing a light bulb into a very big bang?

ALICE: I'm ready.

◆ ◆ ◆ ◆ ◆

SCENE SEVENTEEN

Three scenes on the periphery of the Function Centre.

Murky light.

Sound underneath: a reprise of the music from Scene One; an audience settling, with indistinct talking and muffled coughs; polite rounds of applause; the hum of traffic underneath it all, rising and falling.

ALICE. JIM.

Traffic noise.

ALICE: The door I go in. There's a metal bar across it.

JIM: Not anymore there isn't.

ALICE: Right. Two minutes.

JIM: Yep.

ALICE: As soon as the speeches start.

JIM: Yep.

ALICE: Which pub?

> *Audience sounds.*

JIM: Sorry?

47

ALICE: You said we'd all meet in a week in a pub.

JIM: No. That was them. Not us. We don't have to wait a week. I'm just getting straight on the Number 18 bus. There's a dangerous temptation that kicks in at moments like this. The desire to stay around and watch it happen. Don't give into it. Detonate and go.

He leaves. Music rises, merging into traffic noise.

PAUL. DEBORAH. *He has a tiny bottle, like a whisky miniature.*

PAUL: Why are things different?

DEBORAH: I don't know.

PAUL: Why are we pouring this into a soft drink can instead of lighting the matches on the thing that looks like a birthday cake—

DEBORAH: Put it away.

He does. Audience sounds.

PAUL: Why is it different?

DEBORAH: He said. Jim said. The first lot weren't right. This is easier.

PAUL *looks at his watch. Traffic noise.*

PAUL: Shit. Where's Alice? I don't want to do this. I'm actually not going to do this. I'm not going to do this because I don't know what I'm doing.

Applause. He takes out the tiny bottle, unscrews it and pours the contents on the ground.

DEBORAH: What the fuck is that?

PAUL: Come with me.

DEBORAH: Alice.

PAUL: This is over.

DEBORAH: But Alice—

PAUL: It's too late.

They are gone. The traffic noise, louder.

ALICE. NICK.

NICK: Whatever this is, don't do it.

She stares at him, then turns to go.

I'm going to go inside, Alice. I'm going into the building.

She halts, her back to him. The music and applause, louder.

I'll be in there.

She has gone. The music, applause and traffic noise rise and distort. As the sound reaches a pitch it is vacuumed away with the murky light and we are swept to...

◆ ◆ ◆ ◆ ◆

SCENE EIGHTEEN

Harold's new room. HAROLD. NICK.

Daylight. The sound of a solitary car passing outside. HAROLD *holds a piece of paper. Silence.*

HAROLD: But this just says that I agree to the broadcast. It's a release form. A bit late, isn't it?

NICK: But imagine if you didn't agree. Imagine if you suddenly changed your mind. I would have spent all these hours for nothing. Do you see? Everyone is meant to understand what they're getting into. So release forms are to be signed on day one.

Pause.

HAROLD: You actually tried to get into the building.

NICK: Well yes I did. But I wasn't allowed. I didn't have an invitation. [*Beat.*] So I stood outside and watched it happen. [*Beat.*] People sounded like scalding hot water. [*Beat.*] A guy from the ambulance asked me if I was all right. But I was all right. [*Beat.*] No one else asked me anything. [*Beat.*] I suppose I don't look suspicious. [*Beat.*] There's this guy, Alan, or Aaron I think, from publicity. He wants you to call him. [*Beat.*] There's a lot of interest, you see. They like what they've heard. There are meetings about getting someone to do it all over again for television. You and Bob Hill and Maggie Hutton up at Bob's place.

HAROLD: Hunting for free-range eggs.

NICK: So somebody might be in touch.

Pause.

HAROLD: Have you been to see her?

NICK: No.

HAROLD: I thought I would go tomorrow. [*Beat.*] So you don't know if she's spoken yet.

NICK: No. [*Pause.*] Alan, Aaron, said that Marketing are talking about a book as well. Could I suggest something for the cover. I said probably a photograph at Sophie's.

HAROLD: I haven't seen a paper this morning.

NICK: It's full of words like stable and critical, eight of them are still in hospital. Six, sorry, six. [*Beat.*] But no one seems to have an opinion yet. [*Beat.*] You'll go tomorrow then?

HAROLD: Yes.

NICK: I hope you like the broadcast. I'll send you a tape.

HAROLD: Thank you.

NICK: The room's good.

HAROLD: Once I get a few pictures up. And it's warmer.

NICK: Yes. Yes I can feel that.

Beat.

HAROLD: Do you have a pen?

SCENE NINETEEN

Dual locations: HAROLD *alone.* ALICE *in Remand.*

A scratchy instrumental of 'The Internationale' plays.

ALICE'*s right hand is bandaged. She removes her belt, any jewellery, her wallet, watch and her shoes.*

HAROLD *hands* ALICE *a folded grey, woollen blanket, a sheet and a roll of toilet paper.*

'The Internationale' fades.

HAROLD *addresses his radio broadcast to us.*

HAROLD: It is a simple story. A true story. A story about a woman and a loaf of bread. [*Beat.*] She was the wife of a man who was sacked during the strike. He sat at the factory gates for three weeks while she sat at home. She wasn't interested in politics, she said. Only in feeding her family. Which is why she stole a loaf of bread. [*Beat.*] I defended her, but what could I say? She was fined and released. What I wasn't expecting is that she would walk out of the court and do it again. I watched her. [*Beat.*] She crossed the road, went into a sandwich shop and came out with a loaf of bread. Crossed back over, walked up to the policeman standing outside the court and said: You'd better arrest me. I've done it again.

Remand. DEBORAH. ALICE.

DEBORAH: You can talk. It's only me.

Pause.

ALICE: What happened to Jim?

DEBORAH: I don't know. He vanished. [*Pause.*] Why are you not speaking? You should speak. Have you told them about him? You see I think you should, I think you should tell them everything. Tell them about Paul and me and what we all thought we were doing. If you tell them everything you stand a chance, otherwise, if you just say nothing—When we thought there was something wrong, we wanted to find you, but it was already eight o'clock. We were frightened. [*Pause.*] I'm sorry.

HAROLD *addresses his broadcast to us.*

HAROLD: So she was jailed. Fourteen days. I made a speech outside Fairlea Prison about women who were jailed for loaves of bread. I asked where the new fleet of prison ships was going to be moored. [*Beat.*] And people started gathering. I don't know how. But they were there. It offended them. Punishment for defiance offended them. So they gathered. And they kept gathering.

Remand. ALICE. DEBORAH. PAUL.

PAUL: There's a woman called, I think I've got this right, Najwa? She saw you on the news. She's outside waiting to visit you. She's very angry. She says she can't believe that she lived in bombed-out houses in Lebanon and then finally got to come here

51

and then it turns out her best friend is—. Anyway she's angry. Are you all right?

ALICE: I thought it would be claustrophobic. But I have a bed, a chair, a blanket.

PAUL: What can we bring you?

ALICE: Nothing.

PAUL: Deborah and I think we should talk to the police. Tell them about Jim Morgan. Tell them that he lied.

ALICE: To you. [*Beat.*] He lied to you. [*Pause.*] Do you see?

Silence.

But tell me. Has the world ignited? [*Beat.*] Has everything changed? [*Pause.*] Tell me. Is everything different now?

HAROLD *addresses his broadcast to us.*

HAROLD: And then she was released. But this time with a mission. She would walk from the jail to the gates of the factory and at every possible shop along the way she would steal a loaf of bread. [*Beat.*] But what happened was, she never had to steal. There were about thirty of us now, walking, and people came out of shops and they gave us bread, they gave us cheese, little jars of pickles, whatever they thought they could add. Wine. Butter. Bread. We were staggering with it. [*Beat.*] And alongside us, this little stuttering posse of police and press. [*Beat.*] What did it mean? These people with armfuls of everything? We got to the factory gates and it was just laughter. Bounty and disbelief and you felt, just for a moment, that the world had changed.

Remand. ALICE. NICK

NICK: You're everywhere out there. You're everywhere I look. It's been an avalanche. You're what people talk about. I'm eavesdropping on conversations about you. At first it was confusion, but now it's beginning to sound like hate. [*Beat.*] I'm here, Alice.

He touches her face.

Speak to me. [*Beat.*] Alice. [*Beat.*] Tell me what you're thinking. [*Pause.*] I won't leave you now. [*Beat.*] You have my word.

Pause.

HAROLD *addresses his broadcast to us.*

HAROLD: This feeling that anything was possible. To the freezing, an overcoat. To the hungry, a loaf of bread. This moment. [*Beat.*] Sunlight.

Remand. ALICE.

ALICE: Has the world ignited yet? Has everything changed? Is it all very different now?

HAROLD *addresses his broadcast to us.*

HAROLD: Everyone should feel it once. This moment. [*Beat.*] The promise of a world that might come true. [*Beat.*] This great and simple promise expanding like a star. [*Beat.*] We should all feel it once, this moment. [*Beat.*] When everything is possible, and no one is afraid.

THE END

♟ CURRENCY MODERN DRAMA

The Currency Modern Drama series, edited and introduced by Katharine Brisbane, is a collection of significant Australian plays offering critical and historical perspectives on the development of our contemporary playwriting. There are five books currently available in this series, *Plays of the 60s Volumes 1, 2* and *3* and *Plays the 70s Volumes 1* and *2*, with other books planned covering the 1930s–1980s.

An ideal way to study Australian drama in a particular period, each volume in the series includes a detailed introduction; four to five plays; production photographs and brief biographies of the playwrights.

PLAYS OF THE 60s ▬▬▬▬▬

Volume 1

This first volume of *Plays of the 60s* opens the door to the Australian contemporary theatre and marks its steady urbanisation. In Oriel Gray's study of race relations in a county town *Burst of Summer* we see the culmination of the socialist theatre's 30-year documentation of social issues. Jack McKinney's delightful country comedy *The Well* testifies to the impending end of the cultural isolation of rural life. From Theodore Patrikareas' *The Promised Woman* comes the new world of the post-war immigrant, while Patrick White's radical 'charade of suburbia' *The Season at Sarsaparilla* offers a eulogy to what in the 1950s had been damned as the greatest obstacle to an Australian culture – the inarticulate Australian voice. By the end of the decade, as charted in Volumes 2 and 3, the elevation of vernacular language, begun by White, had achieved heights of peotry and satire not attempted before in Australian history.

0 86819 545 6

Volume 2

The writing here reflects a deep sense of the need for change, and an awareness of the ground beginning to give way beneath the feet. Conscription and the Vietnam War were the major public issues of the 1966 federal election and there was a growing diversity of opinions on the interpretation of history, identity and race. During these years, a truly local form of contemporary theatre began to make itself felt. The sudden spontaneous elevation of language, whether it is used to satirise, to reveal class and credo or to enoble, is a distinctive aspect of these plays.

The plays included are Alan Hopgood's previously unpublished *Private Yuk Objects*, a rich portrait of Australia in the mid 1960s centred around the country's participation in the Vietnam War; *This Old Man Comes Rolling Home*, Dorothy Hewett's celebration of working-class life and politics in inner-suburban Sydney during the Cold War; *The Lucky Streak* by James Searle, a comedy about two inarticulate and aggressive young men who share a room in a boarding house; and *Norm and Ahmed*, Alex Buzo's classic examination of racism and alienation, and the subject of a controversial censorship debate.

0 86819 550 2

Volume 3

In the late 1960s, student revolution spread like wildfire around the world as the post-war generation came to adulthood. In Australia protests against the Vietnam War were mixed with a rebellious new political awareness, and the plays included here reflect the radicalism in public and private life of this period. Each of these works helped advance the horizons of the Australian stage.

The volume features Rodney Milgate's *A Refined Look at Existence*, an ironical comedy drama set in a NSW country town which reworks Euripides' *The Bacchae;* Bill Reed's *Burke's Company*, a study of the explorer Robert O'Hara Burke and his struggle with the Central Australian desert; Alex Buzo's *The Front Room Boys*, a satire set in a government office; and *Chicago, Chicago* by John Romeril, a surreal attack on political exploitation set against the 1968 Chicago Democrat Convention.

0 86819 562 6

PLAYS OF THE 70s

Volume 1

The bicentennial celebrations in 1970 of the arrival of Captain James Cook sparked a reassessment of Australia's history and culture. The plays in this volume were landmarks in the development of a rough new all-Australian theatre which celebrated the rude colour of Australian language and mores. It was a period of comedy and satire; but beneath the larrikinism was a sharp social criticism, which saw ordinary people living alienated, exploitative and largely unexamined lives.

The plays are *The Legend of King O'Malley*, by Michael Boddy and Bob Ellis, which launched Australian theatre in a new direction; *The Joss Adams Show* by Alma De Groen, which examines post-natal depression; John Romeril's *Mrs Thally F,* based on the true story of a Melbourne housewife convicted of murdering her two husbands; *A Stretch of the Imagination* by Jack Hibberd, which was a turning point in the movement against naturalism in its triumphant use of poetry, vaudeville and myth; and *The Removalists,* David Williamson's first internationally performed play, a classic statement on authoritarianism.

0 86819 548 0

Volume 2

The years 1972–75 are remembered as 'the Whitlam period' and the plays of this period reveal a new sense of direction and a need to put the house in order after a brief but heady upheaval. After experiments with social satire, nudity, and challenges to public order, the playwrights here turn to the domestic arena, to examine the way the individual is shaped by society. There is a new preoccupation with personal morality and ethics, and hints of fear and disillusion brought about by change. Peter Kenna retreats to a restricted but more secure society, Alex Buzo wryly questions the advantages of moral freedom, and Jim McNeil and Robert Merritt movingly reveal the toll paid by two of Australia's most deprived communities.

The plays are *A Hard God*, Peter Kenna's classic study of an Irish-Catholic working class family surviving Sydney in the 1940s; *How Does Your Garden Grow*, Jim McNeil's gentle plea from within the prison system that the need for kindness and affection is not confined to those outside; *Coralie Lansdowne Says No*, Alex Buzo's famous critique of the new, liberated woman; and *The Cake Man* by Robert J. Merritt, a simple and moving story of life on a mission in Western NSW, and the first Aboriginal play to enter the repertoire of the white theatre.

0 86819 552 9

Volume 3

Due for publication in May 2001, Volume 3 will feature *The Christian Brothers*, Ron Blair's moving dramatic monologue of a teaching brother grappling with personal anguish and a sense of time departed; *Crossfire*, by Jennifer Compton raises sensitive questions about women's imprisonment and liberation from donmestic structures through a comparison of family life in the 1910s and the 1970s; John O'Donoghue's *A Happy and Holy Occasion* an Irish-Australian portrait full of ebullient humour, guilt and vulnerability and *Inner Voices*, Louis Nowra's exploration of the relationship between speech and thought in the shaping of perceptions.

0 86819 599 5

 Publication of these titles was assisted by the Commonwealth Government through the Australia Council, its arts funding and advisory body.

CURRENCY PRESS
PO Box 2287, Strawberry Hills NSW 2012
Tel: 02 9319 5877   Fax: 02 9319 3649
Web: www.currency.com.au   E-mail: enquiries@currency.com.au

For a full list of our titles, visit our website:

www.currency.com.au

Currency Press
The performing arts publisher
PO Box 2287
Strawberry Hills NSW 2012
Australia

Tel: (02) 9319 5877
Fax: (02) 9319 3649